Copywriting

Everything You Need To Know About Copywriting from Beginner to Expert

Linc Bartlett

© **Copyright 2015 - All rights reserved.**

In no way is it legal to reproduce, duplicate, or transmit any part of this document in either electronic means or in printed format. Recording of this publication is strictly prohibited and any storage of this document is not allowed unless with written permission from the publisher. All rights reserved.

The information provided herein is stated to be truthful and consistent, in that any liability, in terms of inattention or otherwise, by any usage or abuse of any policies, processes, or directions contained within is the solitary and utter responsibility of the recipient reader. Under no circumstances will any legal responsibility or blame be held against the publisher for any reparation, damages, or monetary loss due to the information herein, either directly or indirectly.

Respective authors own all copyrights not held by the publisher.

Legal Notice:

This book is copyright protected. This is only for personal use. You cannot amend, distribute, sell, use, quote or paraphrase any part or the content within this book without the consent of the author or copyright owner. Legal action will be pursued if this is breached.

Disclaimer Notice:

Please note the information contained within this document is for educational and entertainment purposes only. Every attempt has been made to provide accurate, up to date and reliable complete information. No warranties of any kind are expressed or implied. Readers acknowledge that the author is not engaging in the rendering of legal, financial, medical or professional advice.

By reading this document, the reader agrees that under no circumstances are we responsible for any losses, direct or indirect, which are incurred as a result of the use of information contained within this document, including, but not limited to, —errors, omissions, or inaccuracies.

Table of Contents

Introduction 7

Chapter 1 The Evolution of Copywriting 11

Chapter 2 Believing in Your Company's Products 19

Chapter 3 Effective Sales Copy: Copywriting That Hits the Right Spot 25

Chapter 4 The Simple Sales Copy: Why It Sells 47

Chapter 5 The Persuasive Sales Copy According to David Ogilvy 57

Chapter 6 Honing Your Skills for Fun 65

Chapter 7 Use of Different Copywriting Styles 69

Chapter 8 Study of the Competition 75

Chapter 9 How Story Telling is Used by Copywriters 83

Chapter 10 Understanding Your Audience 89

Chapter 11 Continuing with "What's in it for the Consumer?" 97

Chapter 12 What's in it for the Copywriter? 107

Chapter 13 So How Do You Become a Great Copywriter? 113

Chapter 14 Trade Secrets to Effective Copywriting 141

Conclusion 149

Introduction

Knowing more about copywriting may have piqued your curiosity. You may have heard copywriters can make an absolute fortune. Truth is, they can. However, people also have all kinds of misconceptions about what copywriting entails and think they can get by with the average skills of a writer. Unfortunately, that isn't strictly true. Having worked as a copywriter for an advertising company, I know the distinction. I know what holds people back and what makes them a success. This knowledge prompted me to write this book, because there may be a hidden copywriter within you who doesn't know how to express him or her.

This book puts together the different parts of the puzzle so you get a clear picture of what copywriting is all about, instead of just guessing and hoping you can wing it during an interview. Even if you do, unless you have learned the basic rules of copywriting, you won't get far.

From the conception of an idea to the understanding of how copywriting works, this book is a worthwhile investment due to its completeness. You have the choice to take its advice or try to get into copywriting the hard way. It took me a long time to get my head around the way that it works as opposed to traditional text writing. Copywriting is different. The difference between a good copywriter and a bad one can be disastrous for a client and can cost a client business.

If you have been looking at advertisements on the television or in the press, you have been reading copywriting. If a particular advertisement stands out in your mind, then that was good copywriting. Copywriting takes the imagination of the writer a little further because it takes into account the needs of the public, the sector of the public at which it is aimed, and gives them the impression their lives are not complete without a particular product. You may not know it or care to admit to it, but your life has been touched by good quality copywriting.

Have you ever thought about the clarity of a message and how that works in copywriting? You may not have thought beyond writing clever and witty phrases, but you need to. To capture the imagination of the viewing or reading public, you need to go beyond clever and witty into the realms of making the product memorable and that takes a great deal of skill, skill that we will show you how to learn. This book is based upon my experience and I have taken all of the hard work out of the picture, since I have dealt with failure during my own experience and have learned the hard way. You now have all of my information – information that would have made my career as a copywriter much easier, had I known then what I know now.

Taken in small slices, the book shows you all the different aspects of copywriting. With this knowledge, the only way you can fail is if your English is lacking and I assume that you feel, because you are reading this, that you need to take a step further with your writing career, so that's not likely to apply. Copywriting is fun when you get it right and your client is happy. Your words describe your client's product and do it in such a way the product and your client become memorable. Isn't that what all good writers are supposed to do? Keep reading, and I'll explain how to create great copy.

Chapter 1

The Evolution of Copywriting

Everything in the advertising industry is evolving, and so should your copywriting skills. Are you certain your present skills are enough to get customers hooked?

Let's say you surfed online to get information about a car you are planning to buy for yourself but you found no website or welcoming audio, no competitor ads, and no pop-up boxes to be clicked for electronic newsletter subscription. Isn't that frustrating? You would need to take time off work to personally go to a car dealership company yourself to conduct inquiries in order to be informed. Time is too valuable to waste; almost everyone expects to have a map leading them in the right direction and to have access to reliable information regarding the features of the newest car models. Because customers are always pressed for time, it's easier if all those sales policies are already prepared before they even arrive on the site. If these expectations are not met, your eager customer might just visit any one of your competitors.

Effective copy in today's fast-paced world needs to communicate all the key information a customer needs to know without taking up too much of their time. Different mediums for sharing are through text messaging, audio, video, and podcasts—all of which rely on copywriting skills and various techniques to keep up with the times. To put it simply, an effective copywriter must be able to clearly tell their audience what a 40 page sales letter could do in just three punchy sentences.

The significance copywriting plays in the world of advertising has evolved in the last 150 years. Back in 1866, one of the fathers of copywriting, Claude Hopkins, started the idea of researching about consumers prior to writing copy. He also initiated the idea of test marketing before a marketing campaign. In the advertising world today, the Internet has brought about so much change on businesses through the development of websites, SEO, blogging, social networking sites, and e-magazines. These powerful tools have enabled easy communication between producers and consumers, and allowed people the ability to communicate in real time. Our society has rapidly changed because of the technology being introduced. As society evolves, so does the field of advertising. Now, businesses could maximize the use of global communication to tell the world about their products and services. In order to keep up with our ever-changing society, copywriters need to continually adjust to the communication styles technology dictates in order to reach their target market.

What's The Future of Copywriting?

In a study done in 2007 by Robert Half International, copywriting appeared to be one of the top five careers. Skilled freelance and staff copywriters have also increased in number. After the 9/11 tragedy, a lot of people started working from the comfort of their homes in order to regain freedom and control of their time while making a living. Instead of spending most of their time in the office, those who decided to do freelance jobs at home made time to look after their aging parents, take care of their little ones, and even have some leisure time to travel abroad. While this shift happened, entrepreneurs and senior corporate people could not hide how vital it is to produce good copy, creating a high demand for copywriting jobs. During this time, although freelance writing was not something new, it reached its peak supply and demand in high proportions.

The only investment for keeping up with effective copywriting skills against the changing world is continuous training and education. Today, selecting copywriters is based on writing specialties such as within legal, financial, or healthcare fields. Aside from that, another way to preselect the copywriter to fit the bill would be based on the medium that they use: web, white papers, catalogues, etc. Most of the time, it takes time and experience for a copywriter to be a generalist, which consists of getting a few writing gigs here and there while keeping his or her day job.

What Is Niche Marketing?

The launch of new magazines about various crafts and hobbies became widespread in 2006. During this year, about 83 of those magazines focused on specific geographic regions. 59 of them talked about home design and other services, 57 magazines talked about sports, and some 41 magazines were talked about cars. And right after that, poker magazines started to become the craze, with about eight magazines launched in a span of six months. What does this imply? We have so much access to information that consumers are instantly expecting to get their hands on more specific data. Instead of looking for information on how to buy a fishing pole, they would rather read something telling them about the best fishing poles above 5,000 feet.

With all these things in mind, a copywriter who has experience, or even had experience fishing as a previous hobby, would be more adept to connecting with his readers and feed them the exact information they are looking for, even picky ones. Because of this, the trend for entrepreneurs and companies is to search for copywriters who know how to tickle the fancies of their target market. During Claude Hopkin's time, it was close to impossible to be this intimate with his market, but that is not the case in the today's advertising world.

The Science of Copywriting

In one of the previous sections, we mentioned that copywriting is more of a combination of both science and art. In today's world, writing copy is evolving more into a science than an art. This is because today, copy needs to be more susceptible to tests and tweaks. Because of this, marketers are now able to speed up their learning curve when writing the right copy and are able to see results right after a few edits on the copy. Now, marketers are continuously able to innovate through sharing and learning, and others who are new in the business are able to adapt to the learning curve in no time. Consumers have also changed a lot. Now, they are more learned in surfing the Internet and are able to easily distinguish empty copy simply written to make a sale.

According to one of the world's legends in copywriting, Bill Bernbach, "Advertising doesn't create a product advantage. It can only convey it." It's important for marketers to find out which advantage fits their target market in order to captivate them. In this way, it becomes similar to an art. Additionally, advertising is like a science by using tested and proven methods.

Here are some copywriting tips a new-age marketer uses:

Less Formal, More Conversational

Today, marketers do away with a formal writing pattern and have adapted to a relaxed, alternative form. This is because they want to connect more to the reader and the increasing number of younger consumers. Back in the day, copywriters thought it a must to write formally, but this guideline no longer stands. Based on the study done by Forester Research, the trend now is on interactive marketing through emails, SEO, online video ads, and social marketing.

Focus on Benefits vs. Features

To catch the reader's attention, a copywriter must demonstrate in the first two seconds "what's in it for the me [the reader]." WIIFM is the most important ingredient of copy today. Once you are able to connect to the customer you'll catch their full attention, enough to get them reading about the product you are offering.

Aim for Permission-Based Marketing

Customers feel annoyed when you force them into something. Instead of gaining interest, they will ignore you. If they are interested in your product, you will find they listen to you. And once you are able to convey what your product is and what it can do to improve their lives, they will trust your brand. When they do, they tend to willingly subscribe to all your electronic email feed, newsletters, and even download podcasts about your product. This is what permission-based marketing implies.

Include Proof and Validation

A company should always look at testimonials, guarantees, or earned awards as copy must-haves. Customers are wary of scams, fly-by-night businesses, and scandals. They want to be assured trusting your brand will not turn out to be a big regret. It's the marketer's responsibility to make strong guarantees and validations for a sale. For a company website, including other guarantees like staff photos, company history, and information on its relationship with other companies as signs of validation that the company holds a good reputation and stature. If you've got it, flaunt it; because it may be sufficient to provide the proof readers are looking for that you're not just another scam artist.

Indicate Your Promise of Action

In today's fast-paced world, people are looking for instant gratification. How soon will readers shed weight? Can the product be downloaded right away? Is the how-to about the product available in real time? The answers to these questions are what a customer is looking for. And that's what companies need to provide. These are the things your copy should include.

Chapter 2

Believing in Your Company's Products

It's not enough to see a bottle of shampoo and describe it. Advertising is much more subtle than that. The public demands more. If there are similar products on the market, you have to believe that your company's product is better. Not only must you believe it, you must also think of ways in which you can demonstrate it. Copywriting may be limited only to a few words on a television advertisement, a small brochure, or an advert, all of which is very limited in duration. Within a set space of time, you have to produce words people will remember. There are several ad campaigns where this is obvious. Although many adverts irritate the public to the point of turning down the volume, their message is so clear consumers buy into the product, believing it to be better than anything the competition could come up with.

Looking at some everyday examples of popular campaigns that have worked, Head 'N Shoulders is popular all over the world because their copywriters latched onto the fact their shampoo dealt with a problem no one talked about. Everyone else was talking about shine and color, thickness and softness, but no one was actually promoting the idea that dandruff had a cure. Those working on this ad campaign cleverly made a point of not only telling the public about this issue, but of showing them with advertisements that left an impression. You saw the scalp before and after. You learned about the new content of the shampoo and you also learned that compared to other shampoos, there isn't another with the same results.

That's a lot to learn from a two-minute spot on TV, but clever copywriting is what lies behind the best campaigns. A copywriter needs to see an original angle people feel comfortable with. A copywriter needs to believe in the product because that sincerity will show in the words. But it's more than that. They have to come up with ideas as to why one choice is better than another. It isn't enough anymore to have just the brand name of a product, although this helps, of course. Effective copywriting needs to make the consumer feel like they are getting superb value for their money.

In the past twenty years, we have seen great changes in copywriting. There have been televised scripts read by people who were unconvincing, cute animals were introduced into advertising, and even instances where copywriting was creative and amusing. Nowadays, advertising has to have something special that makes the consumer feel his or her needs are being catered to and he or she is being pampered. One of the best lines of copywriting in the last 15 years is the L'Oréal campaign where the key words were "Because you're worth it."

The message you need to get across in copywriting has to be that powerful. When you consider that catchphrase, it was clever because it was aimed toward women who may have thought purchasing expensive items for the sake of vanity should be lower on their priority. However, when people latched onto the catchphrase "Because I'm worth it," millions of women saw another side of the beauty product industry. They began to justify their purchases simply because they began to feel they were special and that the products were specifically made and tailored to their needs.

Believing in the product helps considerably because it gives the copywriter food for thought. Brevity is everything. If you are working on writing words that will appear on a billboard or an advertisement on the side of a bus, people only get a few moments to read it. Thus, lengthy explanations will be wasted. Copywriters produce advertising all around us. If you don't understand the message about the product or event being advertised, the copywriter didn't do a very good job.

As a copywriter, you must take the product, look at it, and consider the best way possible to present the product so the public will see it as advantageous. If you get it right, you will experience success. If you get it wrong, chances are your copywriting days will be short-lived. In the next chapter, we are going to look at successful adverts that won acclaim, as well as look at losing formulas that did not take the public by storm.

Exercise in copyright

Pick up an object in your room and imagine you have to sell this object. Reading over what your message needs to include from the last chapter, close your eyes and imagine words that would make the public know they need that product. Then, instead of using the obvious descriptive words you wrote down for the product, look into alternative adjectives and widen your vocabulary. It's not enough to say something is great. In fact, this may limit the type of market you are trying to impress. Your audience may be more tempted by words such as "innovative" or other adjectives that seem to fit the product. Think of Apple computers and the immediate words one may think of are "crisp" or "sharp." When you begin to think in this manner, it helps you more easily fit the adjectives to products.

Chapter 3

Effective Sales Copy: Copywriting That Hits the Right Spot

Effective sales copy is a combination of art and science rolled. It is considered an art because you need to be creative in order for copy to be perfect. Effective copy has a sense of style and beauty. It also requires you have the proper knowledge of copywriting, the right aptitude, and a certain level of mastery. Copy that follows the art of advertising is useful for content marketing because of its persuasiveness and sense of practicality. It also gives room for its readers to be inspired and captivated.

On the other hand, effective sales copy is also considered a science because of the methodology it follows: the tests, trial and error, breakthroughs, improvements, predictability, and more. Good copy made with scientific methods in mind encourages the development and testing of an idea. That's how you can recognize whether your copy is effective.

Missing one or both of these two makes bad copy. Let's get you familiarized with the many faces of writing copy.

Effective Copy

Plain Copy

Just because your copy is plain doesn't mean it's not going to be effective. Plain copy is the most basic approach in copywriting because it's plain and simple. All it does is introduce the product without the gimmicks, stories, conversation, or exaggerated claims and promises. This type of copy simply presents facts and benefits the product can give its consumers. This kind of copy may not contain all the flowery words worth a literary award but, despite its simplicity, it gets the job done. Try to do this with a household product and see what you can come up with without using flowery descriptions. Plain copy is factual. Make sure to use but increase the level of your vocabulary to make the copy tempting in order to increase the viability of your copy. For this, it may be necessary to invest in a synonym book. There are some rather smart pocket versions on the market.

Storytelling Copy

We are drawn to stories. We love listening to people's lives, histories, challenges, and success stories. We love to hear people's backgrounds, especially when they're interesting. This is because we want to know our similarities. Effective storytelling copy focuses on the moral of the story and uses that part to make the product the catalyst in overcoming any odds.

There are four basic traits that are always present in storytelling copy:

1. Opening: The opening is where the problem is presented. It introduces the pain. It can display the character of the story leading a normal life followed by how things turned around because of a change.

2. Conflict: This tells of the threats imposed on the life of the main character and what happens if he or she does or does not respond properly to the problem. It also tells of the rough journey of the character as he or she takes on challenges.

3. Dialogue: People like the idea of conversations within stories. This shows human interaction at its base roots: talking to one another. People tend to be attracted to dialogue because it is easy to read.

4. Solution: In the end, you need to get to answer the problem. This is where the product is introduced as a cure for the previously presented problem. By doing this, you are raising your product's credibility by sharing detailed results.

Storytelling copy does not need to be dramatic; it only needs to catch the interest of your target audience, which is why it's best to do thorough research.

Exercise: Pick up something in your home or your office and try to create a story scenario useful to promote that particular item. Remember the four elements but also remember your target audience. For example, appeal to parents when you're marketing toys, because parents are the ones spending the money. With baby items, once again, you use the story of parenthood and the dilemmas faced by parents. With more adult items, you need to address problems adults may have and pull these into the story so your product gives the story a happily-ever-after ending. If you want to improve on this kind of writing, you need to improve your story telling skills and get away from corny lines that irritate people. They need to see themselves in the situations you portray. Sometimes advertising fails miserably because it doesn't use the story format effectively.

Conversational Copy

John Caples referred to conversational copy as "You and Me Copy." As its name implies, this type of copy is more like a written conversation between the prospect (the *you*) and the copywriter (the *me*). In writing conversational copy, the language is simple. It's comparable to that of a salesman sitting down with his customer over lunch and discussing a sales presentation. It's straight to the point and identifies with the reader. In conversational copy, it's important to let the reader know the copywriter understands where the reader is coming from, that he or she feels the same, and that picking the product would be the right decision for the reader, as if the copywriter made the same decision to improve his or her own state.

Creating conversational copy is also easier to construct. You don't need to be a seasoned copywriter to create effective conversation copy. In fact, all experience in writing needs to be set aside, as it may dampen the goal to make anything sound natural and conversational. The best way to come up with effective conversational copy is to record and transcribe a conversation about your product.. It's as easy as that.

Exercise: For this exercise, take a household item you really do think you couldn't do without. Record a hypothetical conversation with a friend about this product and then transcribe your words onto paper. Be careful to the extent that the people you are addressing are not close friends. Don't be too personal, but be personal enough so people who read or watch an advertisement containing your copy feel cared for.

<u>Imaginative Copy</u>

In one of John Lennon's famous songs, he persuades us to imagine that there is no heaven, to imagine that above us is only sky, and that there are no countries, no religions, and no wars. Using these words, he is using an effective persuasion tool. This is exactly what imaginative copy is like.

To write this kind of copy as an advertiser, begin with words like "close your eyes," "imagine," "picture this," "pretend for a moment," etc. This type of copy is effective when asking your target audience to imagine a certain status that they want to attain that could only be possible with the use of your product. Using imaginative copy allows your audience to see a vision of their life in a different way: a more improved and upgraded way. Your goal as a copywriter is to paint a picture of how someone's life could be better because of your product.

Exercise: Turn on the advertisements on your TV and watch out for this kind of advert because you will recognize it straight away. It uses the power of the imagination to grab viewers' attention. Now, shut off the TV and imagine a product you want to sell in terms of a fantasy presentation. Try to write out the scenario, bearing in mind this will perhaps be coupled with music but certainly be coupled with imagery. Write down details so you can see the whole thing coming together as a finished project.

Long Copy

The idea behind this type of copy is the more you tell, the higher the chance for you to make a sale. Such copy, with a litany of facts and benefits, are excellent when attempting to convert a customer. Unlike meeting a prospect face to face, a written ad has a single chance to convert its reader. So with long copy, you are laying down all your cards because it's your one and only chance. Using long copy is like answering all the questions a prospective customer may have in mind and writing them down in your copy. This kind of copy actually doesn't follow the pattern of the basic content marketing rules that states you don't have to present all the product's facts and benefits up front. Unlike this type of copy, you have the luxury to divide the content into easily digestible snippets.

If you want to see long copy at work, try accessing the Apple website. You will be greeted by some pretty amazing short copy which catches your attention. Pay attention to examples such as, "The only thing that's changed is everything," which is a powerful message for the iPhone, lulling people who were previously familiar with older iterations of the iPhone into buying the newest version in order to see updates and changes. After, go to a page where you are told more about a product. The long copy goes into the description, but Apple copywriters have taken a very clever way of feeding you into that information. First, you are greeted with catchier short copywriting. In each section, you are encouraged to press for more detail, meaning that Apple website are giving you the choice: either be tempted by the short copy or back up your interest by actually finding out the full details of the item in question.

Exercise in long copy

For this exercise, forget everything you ever read about your telephone. Pick up your cell phone, whatever make it is, and try to write tempting and luring descriptions of the phone that describe what the phone has to offer. Try to be as complex and as intriguing as possible!

Killer Poet Copy

Killer poet copy uses poetry to sell. The goal of killer poet copy isn't to convince its audience that its writer is adept in writing; its goal is to educate and sell using the copy itself. Advertisers who opt for killer poet copy are those who want to maintain style while selling their product. In killer poet copy, the ad is considered an end in itself; it combines creativity with marketing and story with solution.

Exercise in Killer Poet Copy – You may not be the best poet in the world but there is nothing to stop you from trying. Much of the poetry copywriting attempts fails to gain popularity because enough time hasn't been spent on its creation. For this exercise, take a bottle of liquid detergent. Think of a humorous poem that will lull mothers into choosing that kind of detergent because it gives them the enjoyment of reciting the poem to their kids.

When writing poems of this kind, you need to keep the copy relevant to the target market and try to imagine pictures to go with the copy. Remember, there's nothing more irritating than badly scanned verse, unless of course it is done intentionally. Therefore, unless you are going to use this to benefit the copy, keep your verses in scan with the same number of syllables for each line or for alternate lines.

Direct from the CEO Copy

Third party endorsements are a great means to increase sales. However, one should not undermine the impact of direct communication between a product's inventor or CEO and its consumers. With direct from CEO copy, the playing field is how a person of such status could be so down-to-earth as to personally address the consumer. It gives the customers that idea that the CEO is not someone who is cold and inapproachable, but that he cares for his customers.

Direct from the CEO copy can be very plain and conversational. It can be comparable to conversational copy; only it is a conversation between the CEO and the target audience.

Exercise in CEO copy – For this, imagine that you are writing from the stance of a CEO of a large multi-national company. First, write down keywords that help you to decide the message that you are trying to convey. Then work out the sector of the public that you want to convey this message to. For example, if you were the CEO of a popular airline company, you would be aiming the advertisement at potential travelers. The idea of this kind of copy is to take away the distance between the CEO and the target audience. In fact, some of the best copy written in this style was done on entrepreneurs such as Richard Branson and it may be an idea to watch the adverts on YouTube to find out the kind of message that has been conveyed by this type of copy.

Frank Copy

Not all copy talks only about the good qualities of a product. Frank copy, for example, explains ugly things about the product. With this kind of approach, you are not beginning with the charms of the goods that you are selling; you start with its imperfections instead.

By being honest and transparent with your audience about your product, you become more trustworthy in their eyes, making this type of copy effective. And when your audience trusts you, they believe you are being totally honest when stating your product's appeal.

Exercise: For this exercise, take a beauty product you regularly use. Think not only of the virtues of the product, but also accept its inconveniences. For example, a waxing product may work very well but it may hurt some people who use it. Then, open with the inconvenience and work your way through how the product can actually make negative problems easier to handle.

Superlative Copy

Copy can also present extraordinary claims about the product. However, you can only state a superlative claim about your product if you have the proof to back up your claims. Following up your copy with a testimonial, research, or statistics can do this. The downside to using this approach in copywriting, however, is that it's difficult to make such claims without sounding exaggerated. This is the reason why this type of copy is sparingly used.

Exercise in superlative copy: This is the kind of copy that tells you that a product helps you to lower cholesterol. It may be true and backed up by fact. Now, take a product in your home and try to describe it appealingly from statistics you find on the Internet related to the product. It's quite a boring style and people are not that persuaded by it, unless the copy is clever enough to surprise the audience into taking action. Try to make your copy surprising but keep it real.

Rejection Copy

In rejection copy you are trying to distort conventional wisdom by trying to discourage people from seeing your product as something interesting, and instead see it as something else.

With this kind of copy, you are challenging the reader by making them believe only an exclusive set of people are allowed to use y product. Because of the potential rejection, it triggers the reader to be more interested in the product, and piques curiosity in the few people who are qualified to buy the product. Rejection copy approach is best when you want to activate your reader's pride by making them want to belong to a certain status or membership.

Exercise: Look at something you bought because you thought you would never be able to afford it but did. Look at exclusive products you really wanted your partner to buy you and he or she did. Now, look behind the scenes and find out why. Then, take an exclusive product you have in the home and invent a very similar scenario.

Approaches to Copywriting

In the world of advertising, there are many different approaches. Some like to give the impression they have a better product compared to what competitors are selling. But do people really listen to competitors squabbling about who has the best product? Does the public even care? Large supermarket chains realized that it didn't pay off to compare their services with a specific chain. Walmart won't tell you it's better than another specific company. What clever copywriters did was let the public know there is no competitor who can give customers better prices and thus, the price promise begun. Members of the public were told they would be reimbursed if they found cheaper products other than Walmart. This was a very clever marketing tactic, but even cleverer was the way this was worded. Cost-conscious housewives all over the world who were trying to make ends meet were struck by this copy and we can still see its impact today.

World First did a very clever advertising campaign that played on its name as well as using the price promise. When you see the words "World First Price Promise," you think you are being offered an exclusive and exciting deal. In fact, they weren't the world's first price promise at all, but having the name in the sentence made it sound very much as if they were. That's very clever copywriting indeed, and I am convinced many potential customers registered with the company to see what their exchange rates were for different currencies.

There have been some very cleverly worded advertisements that caught the eye of consumers in a big way, so much so that people actually collect them. Do you remember those great Old Spice adverts? Those were good and the writer of the script knew that his or her writing would sell the product. After all, if you can fit everything that interests a typical man into the space of a few minutes, then you really are going to sell to the public. Within a short space of time during the advert, the words used to appeal to a cross section of men included:

Masculinity, Boating, Diamonds, Oysters, Horses, and Pleasing Your Woman

The advert also drew attention to itself by asking viewers to concentrate by repeating the words "Back at me!" This meant that even if a viewer took his or her eyes away from the screen for a moment, they would indeed look back. Old Spice Isaiah Mustafa became renown as the masculinity role model through this advertisement. With its combination of words, voice, and presentation, Old Spice earned a massive eight percent sales increase. Clever copywriting was extremely successful in this particular case.

One of the most memorable advertisements on TV was for the Discovery Channel. Here, the copywriter actually targeted everyone who lives on Earth. The advert, as you may remember, gave the image of two astronauts in space looking toward Earth and saying it made them feel like singing. What followed was a clever advert that extolled all the things people love about the Earth. In its own clever and subtle way, what the advert did was tell the viewing public the Discovery Channel didn't just appeal to one set of people, it appealed to everyone. That was extremely memorable and clever copywriting people actually remember. People continue to think the Discovery Channel as a better option than other channels. It's little wonder that more people tuned into Discovery Channel worldwide to see what it was all about.

Clever copywriting doesn't just mean TV adverts. However, a poll showed people who were actually impressed by a TV advert were more likely to use their mobile device to look up the product they viewed and buy it if they were convinced of the product in question. 28% of viewers said they were more likely to buy something within seconds of seeing an advert if they had a mobile device handy, such as an iPad or smartphone. That means that the sales potential of TV ads is even more powerful than in the days when people needed to remember items when out shopping.

There are many catchphrases people remember from adverts. These are clever because a copywriter has taken a product, come up with a catchphrase associated with it, and essentially conditioned people to remember the catchphrase they've written, although there's no guarantee the person will remember the actual advert years down the line. For example, do these catchphrases ring any bells?

Harley Davidson – American by Birth. Rebel by Nature.

Volkswagen – Think small

IBM – Solutions for a smart planet

PlayStation – Live in Your World. Play in Ours.

Perhaps one of the most memorable, from a family viewpoint, was the slogan used for Kodak cameras, which used the docking system to share photographs.

Share Moments – Share Life

In this catchphrase, there is a lot of clever thought. People were starting to get accustomed to digital photography, but they were still finding attaching photographs to emails complex to a certain degree. The "moments" part of this catchphrase gives the impression the whole process takes moments, or that those captured moments can be easily shared. "Share life" was a clever piece of thinking as well, because it made the whole process of sharing photographs mean more than simply keeping everything in digital format. With people connecting all over the Internet, sharing life made the whole process seem more real. It was a very clever advertising campaign and the copywriting for this catchphrase captured the essence of the product as well as the imagination of the potential buyer.

Yellow pages in the United Kingdom came up with some clever advertising copy as well in their catchphrase:

Let your fingers do the walking.

What they were saying was that often people have to go through loops to get what they want. The advertisements showed different scenarios where people really did have to work hard to get what they wanted, which involved a lot of legwork. The clever use of the fingers being used to access Yellow Pages entries was genius. In the advert, you saw fingers doing the walking instead of feet, and people began to take notice. Why walk when you can simply look something up?

KFC was another company who got it right. What's the first thing you do after you tuck into Kentucky Fried Chicken? Because of its nature, you lick your fingers, so what better way to get the taste buds going than to advertise it as "Finger Lickin' Good?"

Clever copywriting isn't about who shouts the loudest but who can get the public to remember its catchphrase. When I was first in advertising, we were asked to look at ordinary products and come up with unique catchphrases because the company wanted new input. The company wanted to see which personalities fit which contracts. The thinking processes the copywriter goes through encompass:

- Aiming at a particular audience

- Looking closely at what the product offers

- Being able to sum that up in very few words

There were some laughable attempts when we were learning, although as you get into the job, you begin to see things differently. You begin to see what this soap has that others soaps don't. Look at the name "Simple" and in a very clever way, this brand actually gave away the secrets of the soap in its name. It wasn't complex. It didn't include perfumes that may irritate the skin or contents that may leave soreness. It dealt with the probability many people need a soap that does what it says on the label and didn't want to risk allergic reactions. "Simple" said it all.

Blogger's slogan was clever as well. People who were beginning to create blogs were usually not that good with the technical side of blog creation. In fact, the beginner's market was being made to look very simple by the copywriting done for Blogger. If you call something "Push button publishing" it appeals to everyone. It appeals to people in the workplace because it's easy and straightforward. It appeals to the non-initiated because they imagine the pushing of buttons as being simpler than writing HTML, and it appeals to all ages because pushing buttons is something we learn to do from being a child to being a pensioner. That's clever copy!

VISA was another example of great copywriting. Where would you need a credit card? Why would you need a credit card? Would you regret not having a credit card on you? The slogan answers all of the consumer problems concerning credit cards in a simple phrase: "It's Everywhere You Want to Be."

That gives you visions of holidays abroad, traveling to far off places or being in the most stylish of bespoke dressmakers. It's genius; instead of thinking of the ordinary uses of credit cards, the words take you beyond and into the world of fantasy. That's a very clever use of words and imagery because it leaves the viewer of the advertisement with all kinds of pictures in his or her mind.

They used to have an advert where a woman took nothing with her except her plastic tucked into the waistband of her bikini, making you believe the card was all you needed wherever you went. This was clever because subconsciously, you found yourself checking to see if you had your card on you. I know I did, and it was purely in association with the clever catchphrase "your flexible friend." I, along with many others, really did think of my card as a way of being able to stretch my actual cash.

Clever copywriting is the kind easy to remember and leaves you with the feel good factor. Even toothpaste ads are able to make you think positively. The "Colgate Ring of Confidence" may not have been used on adverts for years, but it left its mark on a whole generation of viewers, which is exactly what good copywriting does.

Chapter 4

The Simple Sales Copy: Why It Sells

Leonardo da Vinci once said, "Simplicity is the ultimate sophistication." I totally agree. Why wouldn't I, when even after four hundred years, Steve Jobs, agreed to what da Vinci had said? In fact, it was more than just agreeing, he was so totally sold with the idea he actually plagiarized the advice.

So what is this about? Why would 16th century advice be brought up in the 21st century? The answer is this—simple sells.

According to a book by Handley and Chapman entitled *Content Rules,* "Brevity isn't a luxury; it's a necessity." Furthermore, the book says, "We're in a clarity business, simplifying people's convoluted ideas and wrestling their wild, out-of-control text into something more civilized and comprehensible."

The direction is from transforming something complicated to make it simpler. That is what sales copy should do. We shouldn't confuse would-be customers with all the information of a product and in the process overwhelm them. Instead, the focus should be to make it plain to consumers why they should buy the product and why they must buy it now. Simple sales copy inspires its readers to take action.

So how can we write simple copy that sells?

Concentrate On Just One Goal

Ernest Hemingway said something like this about simplicity, "My aim is to put down on paper what I see and what I feel in the best and simplest way." *Simple* is to one as *complex* is too many. One of the distinctions between simple sales copy and complex copy is in the number of goals. When you are concentrated on just one goal, you can keep your copy short, specific, and simple. Having too many goals, on the other hand, takes up a lot of explaining and detailing in your sales copy.

When writing simple copy that sells, you have to discipline yourself to concentrate on just the call to action, or what Dan Kennedy refers to as the "strategic purpose." He shares that though he may have lots of ways to get clients to inquire about his services, each way has its strategic purpose. And you must understand your purpose for each piece.

Focus On One Audience

Another quote on singularity from William Shakespeare,

"Therefore, since brevity is the soul of the wit

And tediousness the limbs and outward flourishes,

I will be brief: your noble son is mad."

We talked about the importance of singularity in purpose. It's about the importance of having only one audience.

In sales and marketing there is what you call the 80/20 rule, which basically states 80% of your sales is actually from only 20% of your customers. As an entrepreneur, you need to focus on that profitable percent of customers in order to result in a bigger sale. When writing simple copy that sells, you need to qualify your audience by narrowing your focus down to the 20% who will give you that potential sale.

Converse, Don't Narrate

Have you noticed in most of the errors we have in print, we are able to avoid in conversations? This is especially the case when we are trying to impress people with big words. You know why this happens? It's because we just flow when we converse. We become spontaneous. We don't complicate our sentences and we choose simple and plain words. When we converse, we want our listener to easily understand us and to keep the rhythm of communication. More so, when we talk, we do it without even giving it much thought. We don't struggle much in selecting our words; they just flow forth informally and naturally.

To do away with complexity, use conversation as a tool when creating simple copy that sells. After writing down your copy, enlist the help of an editor to read your copy out loud, or record your voice reading your copy out loud. Edit out parts that sound unnatural for one person to say to another.

Avoid Mentioning Jargons

Albert Einstein said, "If you can't explain it to a six-yearold, you don't understand it yourself." To make simple copy means it is devoid of all the insider words people outside the company would not understand. Every one of us struggles with insider vision, which shouldn't be the case when we are talking about sales copy. If you want people to really understand what your product can do to improve their lives, you need to let them in, and not let them get caught in your curse of knowledge.

To write simple copy that sells, insider vision and insider language should be forever banned. If you can't help it, you may use big words in your copy, as deemed appropriate, but always remember to explain them if needed.

Decrease Your Use of Adjectives and Adverbs

If you want to simplify your copy without doing much harm on content and impact, cut your adjectives and adverbs in half. For one, they don't add information; they take up too much of your space and make your copy dull.

Jerrod Morris was moved by Stephen King's lack of belief in adverbs, as shown by his statement: "Write what you mean and mean what you write. Use adverbs where they are pretty and unique in their boldness. Then, and only then."

Cut Until It Hurts

According to Jony Ive, simplicity is more than just a visual style. Being simple is not just about ridding clutter and being minimalist. Simplicity goes as far as digging deep until you have uncovered complexity.

Exercise at improving your copy: In this exercise, we need you to write copy for advertising something you have in your home. Write copy of 200 words. Now, imagine your chief of staff has asked you to cut this down to 100 words and do a precis of the written work you have done. Precis is one the best friends of the copywriter and if you don't know how to do it, it's time to learn because using it will make your copywriting slick and less will indeed say more.

As you simplify your sales copy, you will come to a point of stripping it to the point that it's left only with what is essential to the product. Sometimes you have to give up a sentence you so loved, or a phrase that took you so long to construct, or a paragraph that really sounded clever and edgy but really did not add any value. It hurts, but that's the mark indicating you are on the right track.

George Orwell shares this list, which can be used as a cheat sheet on creating simple copy that sells:

- Use a word for a phrase

- Use a phrase for a sentence

- Use a sentence for a paragraph

- Use a paragraph for a page

I believe even seasoned copywriters would agree good copy is not measured in how tacky sales copy is written. It also cannot be counted as better copy if only a highly intellectual can understand it. Simplicity is the goal of all good and persuasive copy. The clearer, the shorter, and the easier to understand, the better. People are wired to get to know, like, and trust things that are clear and simple. Clear and simple are the right ingredients for making a sale. As Perry Marshall says, "You should always be suspicious of complicated things. You should be even more suspicious of people who make simple things complicated."

Exercise in Brevity: Your audience is comprised of late teens in the workplace. These are young people who have a regular income and you are trying to sell them the idea of a space saving device in which they can carry all of their technology. Write the copy with this audience in mind and a full description of what you are offering them and at what price. Now, pick out keywords from your writing. These are words that will stay in the mind of the reader. Highlight them within your text. If you are keyword stuffing, people will notice. Add up the number of words in your copy and divide by 5%. If you have more keywords than that, you are using too many and are guilty of keyword stuffing. If your percentage is too high, knock out the words you believe to be less effective and rewrite those sections in order to knock your percentage below 5%.

Now, try this from a story telling perspective. Use the same product and keep in mind your keywords should be less than 5% of your copy. Carefully think of a scenario. Remember, the product itself isn't the object of your writing. The object is to sell the product to the previously discussed age range because THEY NEED IT.

Write down all the reasons you think these kids need the product and how you think it will improve their lives. Then, work on keywords. These should be relevant words to kids of this age. If you were to tell a teen something is "groovy," they would likely think of it as outdated and more in line with their parent's thinking, if they were to understand the adjective at all. Thus, use adjectives carefully when describing what the product will do for the teen. Make it snappy, relevant, and conversational. Copy such as this shouldn't be condescending. For example, teens may not want advice from a parent or anyone else because they feel as though they understand the world well enough to know themselves at this stage in life. Therefore, a teen would not be able to see copy with advice as conversational. Thus, try to imagine one teen talking to another. Use this to come up with your storyboard of ideas, and then finish writing the copy needed to convey your message to the public.

Once you have written the copy, work out the percentage of keywords and cut back the text to half its original length. The idea of playing around with copy is to get you familiar with the process so these processes become automatic so you can easily improve your copywriting skills. The better you get at conveying your intended message; the more likely your copy is to actually interest your targeted audience in your product. You need to prove yourself. Having some examples of copy you can show to a prospective client will help you gain more work, especially if the potential client likes what they read. Keep it fresh and new and if you think you are entering hackneyed territory, rewrite and start the process again.

Chapter 5

The Persuasive Sales Copy According to David Ogilvy

David Ogilvy is one of the masters of advertising. He is often referred to as the Father of Advertising, being the one who successfully founded Ogilvy & Maher. Aside from fathering a multibillion-dollar company, he is also the man behind successful advertising campaigns for other market giants such as Rolls Royce, Dove, and Shell.

If you are aiming at mastering the art of creating persuasive copy, David Ogilvy is the man to follow. A lot of people have been inspired to improve the way they create copy by watching David, and following what he says in his book. Here are a couple of things we can learn from the advertising guru:

> *Don't bunt. Aim out of the ballpark. Aim for the company of immortals. – David Ogilvy*

You have to go big; otherwise, just go home. When writing copy, always think big. Don't create copy for the sake of writing copy. Your copy represents the brand you are selling. You cannot afford to take shortcuts or present something you know is not compelling. If you believe you are selling something great, your product doesn't deserve bad copy. Now, if you are not skilled enough to perfect the copy for your product, hire someone who can.

> *Advertising people who ignore research are as dangerous as generals who ignore decodes of enemy signals. – David Ogilvy*

Don't depend on your finite knowledge. It is okay to admit you don't know everything. Do your homework. If you are not confident enough about what you know, research. Even Ogilvy invested years of work for George Gallup of Gallup Poll. With the amount of time he spent there, he realized the importance of knowing what your target audience actually has in mind. Three vital things you need to answer when writing copy are:

- Who is it for?

- How do they think?

- What do they need?

Without really finding the answer to these questions, you are just merely assuming and faking the process. And guess what? You'll come up with exactly the kind of copy that will get you in deep trouble. The secret to writing great copy is having this in mind: "I want to understand my audience so I can serve them better."

> *A customer is not a moron. She's your wife. Don't insult her intelligence, and don't shock her. – David Ogilvy*

Don't belittle your customers. When writing copy, you are not supposed to speak in a tone that assumes the audiences you are talking to are stupid. You can educate your audience through copy but not to the point of condescension. No matter how good your intentions may be, speaking to them in such a manner is only going to chase them away instead of attract them. Persuasive copy allows its readers to see the product as there to help them solve a problem. But then, make sure to leave your customer dignified and respected. At the end of the day, it is you who will benefit most from a sale.

On the average, five times as many people read the headline as read the body copy. When you have written your headline, you have spent eighty cents out your dollar. – David Ogilvy

A headline is like a preview of the entire copy. If you are going to show all your cards, it should be at this point. If you are able to get your audience with a strong and catchy headline, then you succeeded in catching your customer's interest. If your copy is worth a dollar, the impact of the headline is worth eighty percent of that. How can you make your headline worth the read?

- Select from headline templates, which are actual headlines that have worked before.
- Make headlines that stress strong benefits in order for your reader to want to read more.
- Do a split test to see which headlines work best for your target market.

If it doesn't sell, it isn't creative. – David Ogilvy

Sometimes trying too hard to be innovative, funny, and original can be a little dangerous. Because of trying so hard to make your copy perfect, it becomes the very reason you get distracted from making a sale. Remember, copy is just a tool to reach your aim, which is a sale. People don't allot time for just reading ads. Time is precious. Everyone is always in a hurry. If your copy doesn't clearly state the point, he or she might never have the luxury to read it again. Then, all your effort is in vain. If you want a sale, allow your customers to visualize how it can improve their lives. That should be the purpose of your copy; everything else is just secondary.

> *The more informative your advertising, the more persuasive it will be. – David Ogilvy*

Always explain the reason why your customer should buy the product you are advertising. Don't emphasize so much on the *what*; let them know the *why*. Now that you caught their attention using your headline, don't bombard them with so much information describing the product. They are not going to buy just because they know that the product is. What's going to make them decide to buy is if they understand the importance of the product in improving their lives. When writing persuasive copy, highlight:

- Why the product is important
- Why buying the product is a good deal

- Why your customer should buy the product from you
- Why your customer should buy your product with urgency
- Why your customers should place their trust in you

Feed your customers the answers to these questions and you'll see, consciously or unconsciously, taking in all of this information is like filling up all the questions in their heads. And when you have done so, the only thing left for them to do is act.

> *Like a midwife, I make my living bringing new babies into the world, except that mine are new advertising campaigns. – David Ogilvy*

Convince yourself of the importance of your copy. Never treat sales copy as an afterthought. Don't just scribble some notes, grammar check it, and send it out. If this is your process, no wonder you can't get the results you are looking for.

David Ogilvy shares that he treats every one of his campaigns as though they are his babies. Just like his own children, he nurtured them, stood up for them, and helped them grow. And look how far his campaigns have reached in the realm of advertising history. Great copy is the fruit of much effort and sacrifice. The best copywriters are often those who have willingly invested weeks of hard planning just to craft a headline, and months to produce body copy. It's not because they lack the skill or that they are slow, but that they know how important it is to get it right.

Chapter 6

Honing Your Skills for Fun

The next time you find yourself sitting in front of the TV, look at the adverts and work out which are clever copywriting and which are simply mediocre. Then, switch off the TV. Copywriting is a matter of practice. It's a matter of being able to be astute with a few words. It's making a short description of something while encompassing all of the benefits of that product in the right kind of wording aimed at the sector of the public for which it is intended.

Pick up a product within your home and take out your notebook. The first thing we were always taught to do was decide in simple terms what the product is, what the product does, and whom it is aimed toward. That gives you an idea of the kind of wording that appeals to consumers.

For example, when appealing to businessmen or people about technology, you need to use words they might associate with technology. Keep it slick, simple, and to the point. Copywriting is clever. It doesn't use so many words so that people can't relate to it.

Look at the IBM quote in the last chapter. It does all of this and also encompasses including those people who are conscious of the Earth and the environment. Now, try writing down adjectives that describe the product. For example, I am going to describe a handbag, as this is what is in front of me:

Stylish

All encompassing (should be – it carries everything)

Quality

These few words just about sum it up and I don't need to add much more. I have said it is quality, I have said that it carries everything and I have said that it's stylish. Due to these elements, this should appeal to a practical woman, a style-conscious woman, and a woman who likes to think that she buys quality items.

Now, try this with your product and see what you can come up with. You have to practice to be good at copywriting, but you need to be a little flexible as well. Perhaps you can specialize in cosmetics or something with a lot of different lines, but if you end up working as a freelancer for an advertising company, the chances are you will be asked to write copy for all kinds of products, so the more practice you get, the better.

I used to sit and scribble for hours when I was waiting for doctor's appointments or waiting for a bus. It helps to widen your vocabulary and to be able to play on words, so get in as much practice as you can if you want to be a great copywriter.

Chapter 7

Use of Different Copywriting Styles

The idea of this chapter is to take you back through different styles, so you will need to go back to the styles chapter and work out which style is suitable for the product you are about to describe. I have chosen an obscure cross-section of items because this gives you good practice at getting the right style, which is what copywriters do to increase their adaptability. Look at the items below and decide upon the audience to whom you should be addressing your copywriting.

Think to yourself:

- What's in it for the client?

- What kind of client do you think you are aiming at?

- What does the product offer that others don't?

Product 1: Ready meals – These are pre-prepared meals with good nutrition in mind. When you get the parcel, you get all the ingredients you need to make the meal plus a recipe so you have everything you need for a set amount of people.

Product 2: Gravy granules – These are an instant gravy product that produce a gravy by adding hot water.

Product 3: The latest sports car – In this case, you can choose the vehicle because your copywriting is hypothetical. It should be a popular brand. Regardless of your choice, title the piece so you know exactly what car you are trying to sell.

Product 4: A plush teddy bear – In this case, the teddy is a well-known one and responds to cuddles with a gentle growl.

Product 5: An anti-aging treatment for the skin – This is at a lower cost than normal treatments, which may widen your potential audience.

Product 6: A computer for the computer-illiterate – Brought onto the market for those who are having trouble becoming familiarized with technology.

For each of the above scenarios, first determine the age range of the people to which your copy is being directed. You may even want to state an income range so you can learn more about those people and what it is they are seeking. Knowing your audience is everything.

Next, determine the length of the copy and its use. For example, will this be an advertisement with images? If so, what kind of images do you imagine with your words? Work out the format of the copy and give yourself a word limit and a keyword limit for your work.

Then, look at the styles section of this book and work out which style you think would work best with the product. You can call your product anything you wish since this is hypothetical, but decide what type of copy will attract the right kind of audience to tempt them into buying the product.

Writing the copy

Remember, it's vital you show consumers how this product will improve:

- Their lifestyle
- Their ease of living
- Their status

You need to write the copy within the guidelines you have given yourself. For each product, close your eyes and try to come up with a catchphrase. Remember, you don't have to use adjectives. Let the product speak for itself. For example, we all know the advertisement "Beanz meanz Heinz" or "Because you're worth it." Try to come up with a catchy phrase people will remember when they think of the product you are writing about. These catchy phrases are what pull people into buying your product; therefore, they are very important. Write this into the copy at some stage where it makes an impact and highlight it as your slogan. Keep a notebook and if you think of slogans, even for items you have not been asked to do any copywriting for, these can come in handy inthe future.

Getting better at writing

To improve your chances as a copywriter, you need to learn to self-edit. Put your work away overnight and do not think about it anymore. The next day, take your work out and read through it, editing it and making it better. Often, copywriters who are too hasty when submitting their copy regret they did not tackle the job differently. Don't regret your work. Edit your copy. Look at your slogans and see if you are happy with what you produced.

If you are new to the copywriting scene, you may be able to use such examples to demonstrate to a future employer that you do have ideas and you are able to work within the discipline they demand. All of this will help to advance your career.

Chapter 8

Study of the Competition

Good copywriters are able to poke holes in the competition. They look at the products, try them, and compare them. One thing they look for is the weaknesses of the competition because those weaknesses help the copywriter to come up with strengths when describing their own products. They know the public will also be aware of those weaknesses and don't need to resort to name-calling in order to get across a message.

It's worthwhile looking at all types of advertising. Watch TV adverts, read adverts in magazines, and understand the subtlety being demonstrated. If one product claims to do one thing, yours needs to not only do that one thing, but it needs to offer even more. If you don't exploit your competition's weak points then you are not doing a very good job as a copywriter. I remember seeing an advertising campaign for an airline company whose prices were quite expensive. This was at a time when "no frills" airlines were pouting about being able to get people from A to B in a very short amount of time without charging for all the "frills." What came to mind instantly was all the complaints recently shown on TV about budget airlines. Thus, exploiting the competition's weakness was actually very easy. Their weakness was what they actually saw as their strength. Not everyone wants to buy everything on the cheap and some travelers prefer the luxury and comfort of being pampered. After all, how often do you go on vacation? In this situation, the ideal copywriting for advertising the more expensive airlines would use words such as, "Exclusive, Customer Care, Comfort, Space," as opposed to the ideas people were gleaning about budget airlines.

There was a spate of complaints about cabins not being clean, about turnovers being too rapid, and about the amount of hand luggage customers were permitted. On luxury flights, no such restrictions existed. There were no extra charges for extra baggage and although prices were more expensive, the holidays offered luxury cabins with plenty of room to move and there was consistently the best customer service that could be offered.

It's important to understand copywriting is about encompassing the message of the company in a short space of time in order to be more memorable than the competition. When a consumer is faced with multiple choices, they are more drawn toward purchasing an item they feel is familiar. That familiarity may just have happened because of clever copywriting, rather than the fact anyone had recommended the product or the consumer had ever used it before. Good copyrighting has to include the following elements:

- The usefulness of the product
- The strength it has against the weakness of competitors
- Why people should buy it or trust the name
- A convincing argument in favor of the product

If any of these elements are missing from the advertisement written by the copywriter, it can mean the company will lose out on potential profits. So, as you can see, it's not about writing a simple description of a product. It's about understanding the ideology behind it, the strength of the product and the weaknesses of competition. Thus, it's not straightforward writing and if you think it is, you may be looking at the wrong career.

Copywriting is clever wording. You see it on street adverts. You see it on neon signs but unless it's astutely written, the message it gives you is not memorable. That's why people are prepared to pay copywriters good money. They know it means the difference between getting the message home to the public and actually missing the point, which could cost the company a lot of revenue.

You also need to remember you need to appeal to the sector of society at whom the product is aimed. In some cases, advertisers use very odd tactics. In a particularly successful campaign to get people to borrow money, the copywriter thought about people's feelings about loan companies. They called them loan sharks. They looked at the amount of interest these companies charged before actually thinking of them as being viable alternatives. In the Wonga.com advertisement, they showed a group of old people past retirement being the lenders, thus gaining the trust of the public because they wouldn't think of these elderly people as being capable of cheating them.

Thus, the company grew in strength and the advertisements became more regular so people also saw the chance of borrowing money as being a viable option to get them through hard times. Wonga.com made it look easy for consumers to get their hands on money but they appealed to the middle class or working class public. They also used the slogan "Fast Little Loans," thus trivializing the fact people had to borrow money to survive.

There are many examples of the best adverts and also the worst adverts you can see on websites such as YouTube, but remember that copywriting was involved in all of them. If a company failed, chances are the copywriter was not successful at putting out the message the company wanted him or her to and the public didn't actually enjoy or receive any positive message from the adverts.

I remember all kinds of advertisements over the years, though those that stand out had a dialog with which I felt comfortable. That's what it's all about. It's not enough anymore to send a subliminal message through advertising and those that attempt this don't always deliver the message they intended. However, clever copywriting will always get good results and that's what people pay copywriters to produce – results that show a rise in profits.

Even manufacturers themselves are listening to what the public thinks of their products and are using this in their copywriting. For example, at one time it was so expensive for people to buy ink cartridges that advertisers started to make the point their systems offered the client the potential of less expensive ink. A good manufacturer learns from experience and it's a good practice to look at two products, one being a dated release and one being a new release, then write copy for both as an exercise in how you sell someone something that they potentially already have.

In this case, you don't need to go very far to find products. For example, items like iPhones or certain tablets have produced updated versions that offer the consumer more than the original may have offered.

Exercise in updating the specs on a new product

This kind of copy is very relevant. You are aiming at the same target audience, but you are trying to tell them the product they originally bought is now outdated. Take, for example, an iPad and for the first copy, use an older model and write up copy as if this were the new iPad. Your advertising copy in this case would have been released at the same time as the old release of the iPad, so it is a bit retrospective, but there is a very good reason for doing this. Once you are happy with the copy, have checked the keyword density and have cut it down to a minimum, access a page which describes a new iPad and do the same thing, bearing in mind you don't want the customer to feel like he has been ripped off and you are now offering something that makes his old iPad seem a waste of money.

Technology is ever-changing but copywriting rules don't drastically change. Thus, in this exercise, your two chosen gadgets are things that have been updated and improved as technology grew and advanced. Since this is a high turnover area of the market, your exercise won't be wasted. You will be able to demonstrate to someone looking for high tech copywriters how you distinguished between old and new models while making both look appealing at the time they were released. In this day and age, an exercise such as this just may gain you a new client and will also give you the practice you need in order to deliver high quality, innovative copy.

Chapter 9

How Story Telling is Used by Copywriters

Storytelling achieves many aims. It helps a potential consumer to be able to feel comfortable with a particular product or with a particular storyline so they will go out and buy the product. Several very successful adverts come to mind when it comes to storytelling. One was based in an old town in Italy and showed the male in the story as being very versatile, even though he was of advanced age. The message behind this story was that if you use olive oil, you are likely to have Italian stamina. It was an amusing storyline and one that got viewers suffering from middle-aged spread to actually go out and buy the product in the hopes it could at least give them some stamina like the old man in the storyline.

Other advertisements that come to mind are those used by ComparetheMarket.com. They got people to remember the name "market" by cleverly introducing characters who were Meer Kats. In order to make the Meer Kats sound like they were saying Market, they had to introduce an accent and in doing this, created a whole list of Meer Kat characters people started to collect. Such was the success of the Meer Kat adverts people began to collect soft toys given when you took out business through the website. People were also bought books from Amazon that told stories of their favorite Meer Kat characters.

Storytelling has been used in many advertisements. When Dodge aimed its new truck at the farming community, it did it in style with the "God Made the Farmer" advertisement. The story went into all the roles farmers are expected to perform, even though these are sometimes hard and beyond the scope of most people. Farmers could relate to what was being said because the words actually applied to them. Although the emphasis was on the role of a farmer, the message of the advert was quite clearly geared at upping the amount of revenue Dodge would be able to make from its new truck and it worked. This was a clever copywriting idea that took farming back to its basics and saw the role of the farmer in such a valuable way that every farmer or would-be farmer who saw it could easily see the special relationship farmers have with the land he tends and the herds he oversees.

Taco Bell did a great story and it wasn't cleverly acted but the copywriter came up with a unique tease to Taco Bell's competitor, McDonalds. They chose people to appear in the advert who had the name Ronald McDonald. These people would try out the Taco Bell breakfast treat and extol its virtues. It was a little like a play on words but in a very unique way. This fun-filled advert caught the imagination of viewers and was one of the most successful storytelling adverts because of this.

Storytelling pulls at the heartstrings of viewers, which in turn pulls at their purse strings. In a Cheerios advert, for example, a young child gets into a situation where his father is never around at breakfast and is forever working the late shift. When the father comes home in the middle of the night, his son is at the fridge. He asks what he's doing up at this time of night and the child answers he just wants to have breakfast with his dad. Family stories make great advertising because this is the target for breakfast cereals and this advert gained popularity not only because it was a heartwarming father/son story against the backdrop of hard work, it was also successful for the company.

If you can incorporate a story, it may work in your copywriting. Although there are times a catchphrase may be all that is needed when you want to capture a specific audience, storytelling is more likely to get attention. People particularly like a story that gives them a really happy feeling, such as the advert mentioned above. However, watch out for the weak stories, as these are unlikely to earn accolades for the copywriter who produced them.

Exercise in story telling

For this exercise, I want you to imagine you are selling life insurance to seniors and come up with a story that will back up their need to have life insurance. Remember, add keywords, make sure you don't keyword stuff, and edit your copy when you have finished. Make this a set 150 words. The story should appeal to seniors and make them face the responsibility that they may not be here to see their grandchildren grow up. Let your imagination loose and write your story, making them feel comfortable they have their options covered and that they will not become a liability to their children in the event of the unfortunate happening. Be forewarned: this has been done before so don't copy ideas. Make yours original.

Now, try to tell the story to younger people, aiming at selling life insurance to them. In this case, you have the backdrop of people thinking they won't ever need life insurance, so your story has to take this into account and show there may come a time in the young person's life when life insurance really can be useful.

Chapter 10

Understanding Your Audience

There is an audience for cheap and cheerful products. Thus, advertising for this sector of the market may mean you have to get to that level of thinking to actually win customer loyalty. Many supermarkets do this because they put themselves out as family-friendly and families in this sector of society want to save money. In fact, by the time they have scouted around the supermarket, they may have spent much more than they intended, which was the purpose of the advertising drive. There have been loads of advertising campaigns that offer the customer a refund of the difference if the goods are found cheaper elsewhere. Of course, that promise may be something a fussy customer would ask the company to do, but for most, the promise is enough to tempt them to buy within that environment, trusting the company had already done its research and wouldn't be putting itself on the line for no reason.

There are several sectors you may be aiming at and some of them are shown here:

- Seniors who are well off
- Seniors struggling to make ends meet
- People with infirmities
- Middle class families with medium income
- Upper class families with little financial constraint
- Upper class students with family money
- Students struggling to keep up with peers
- Children

Of course, these groups can be split into even more sectors, but the basics are there. Seniors with plenty of money will be only too happy to part with it for grandchildren or for their own comfort. Those with less are likely to still need things that help with health issues or with insurances because they worry about things to come.

The child market is amazingly lucrative because if you aim for the heartstrings of kids rather than parents, the kids do the rest of the work for you. Parents want their kids to have their favorite things. Be aware that copywriting in these areas is particularly rife with competition and that it isn't enough anymore to depend upon reputation.

The advertisers of laptops and tablets, for example, need to come up with exciting, inventive things and the advertising campaigns of top competitors is staggering. Read adverts and you will see exactly what I mean. The Samsung ATIV is a typical example. This was aimed at families and starred a baby. The narration was done as if the child was talking. This was clever copywriting because it made the accessibility of the tablet something that improved the lives of the child's parents. The copywriter also used the name of the tablet in three descriptions, the name being ATIV:

- CRE**ATIV**

- INNOV**ATIV**

- ORIGIN**ATIV**

Thus, potential purchasers were given prompts to remember the model. That's clever copywriting and would have captured the hearts of buyers within richer family environments. Working parents with kids at daycare would have remembered that advert. That's a good target market because there's money to spend.

Apple iPad copywriters came up with the equation of using the word "delicious" to introduce their product and followed it with a storyboard aimed at all different markets. It was a very clever advertisement that appealed to children, socialites, networkers, and entertainers, and it did so in a way that encouraged everyone to see the iPad as offering opportunities to learn, play, read and many other things. In a later advertisement for the new iPad, the script was instantly a hit with everyone and was cleverly aimed at a wide audience.

It started with the words that drew people into the advert:

"We believe technology is at its very best when it's invisible."

It's only a short phrase but it's one that instantly draws the attention of a technophobic and those a little scared of change. With so much criticism being leveled at people's new ways of communication, iPad went one step further. It showed how the iPad could be used in the background of life, rather than becoming life. That was a win-win in advertisement because even parents who may be a little against children locking themselves away with technology could see the social aspects of using the iPad.

As you can see from the small demonstrations given in this chapter, copywriting isn't about describing a product. It's about describing what the product can do for you. In order to do that correctly, you need to know your target audience. Then you can write copy aimed at a particular audience to make the campaign more successful.

It's a very good idea to see what's currently trending and to look at examples of successful advertising campaigns. These will be for products you are familiar with but you must ask yourself why you are familiar with them. Have you used them? Have your friends used them? Perhaps you were simply targeted by clever copywriting but haven't yet quite made the decision to purchase. If you remember the name of the product and its price, then chances are the copywriter did a good job of advertising . Clever bylines that target the audience are wonderful and that's something that needs a very unique approach indeed.

Exercise in understanding your audience:

For the purpose of this exercise, we ask you to take a product and imagine the markets you are aiming at. Instead of this being one specific market, imagine marketing to three sectors of society. Then produce copywriting that addresses each, bearing in mind the product is the same but the market is different. What this exercise does is help you to see how your wording and the way you present the product will have an impact your audience as it changes, even though the product is exactly the same. The way to address this is to identify the three sectors of society first. Then, write a list of keywords that show you what that particular cross section of society would want to gain from purchasing the particular product. I can make this explanation easy by using something of universal appeal. In this case, let's use a standard tablet. The three sectors of society that I want to aim the copy at are:

- Seniors with a lot of money
- Seniors with limited income
- Parents of young children

Although these are three different sectors, you need to find out how each sector would regard the product as beneficial. Remember, they will be asking "What's in it for me?"

Seniors with a lot of money – Instant access to a multitude of apps. The potential to link gadgets and the portability of the product.

Seniors with limited income – The opportunity to buy online and save money. Less need to get out in the world because of being able to keep in touch by Skype. Ease of use.

Parents of young children – Learning potential for kids. Ease of use. Ability to help children keep up with the modern world.

From the example I have shown you, you can see each set of people has their own priorities. This is what you need to capture when you are aiming your copy at a particular sector of society. Now, choose a product and do the same thing by writing out your copy to hit the right market. Then, check your work and edit it the next day. Try to conform to a standard wording amount for each, for example, try 250 words.

To improve your ability to be astute, knock the word count down to 150. This helps you to learn the importance of brevity. People only watch or read an advert for a few moments. Thus, if your copy does not make them sufficiently curious about the product, you will have failed. The practice of precis is going to be your best friend, so whenever you get an opportunity to practice your writing skills, always write more words than you need and make precis a part of the job. If you do this, you will naturally edit your copy as you go and will find you really can get the message across with a punch!

Chapter 11

Continuing with "What's in it for the Consumer?"

The consumer will always be hungry to consume, but they also need to feel singled out and special. If an advertiser is aiming their product at an individual, then the copywriter needs to remember each member of the audience is an individual who wants to feel the message him or herself. Thus, you need to answer the unasked question of "What's in it for me?"

In the above examples, for instance, iPad made the experience extremely personal. The copywriter was very particular about using the word "you" because this was intended so each viewer developed personal feelings about the iPad. It wasn't marketed to the masses by simply using "we" or "the buying public." Instead, it captured the imagination of viewers in a storybook way that encompassed things that would be great for:

- o Kids
- o Adults
- o Learners
- o Gamesters
- o Readers
- o Movie buffs
- o Photographers

The best thing is that the advertisement actually showed each of these people what was in it for them. That's wonderful advertising. Kids had no question that they wanted the iPad. Adults knew it was better for their eyes because of the retina display. Learners were shown how much information could be gleaned, so they had a fair idea of how much use they get out of an iPad. In fact, every group that was advertised toward had personalized images to make them feel like the iPad met their needs so there was absolutely no question about what was in it for them.

Another great advertising campaign is the Dyson adverts. Women and even men are left with no doubt Dyson has provided innovations that makes housework much easier. No one can be in any doubt knowing that owning a Dyson product means a cleaner house with less work following Dyson adverts. That's what is in it for purchasers and it's a pretty desirable thing for consumers to grasp even though the prices are expensive. Dyson shows you technology that makes you believe their product is better than the competition, thus exploiting competitor's weaknesses and justifying the hefty bill paid to own one.

When copywriting, the write up should leave absolutely no question as to what's in it for the purchaser, but it has to be based on truthful claims or it will backfire. Garcinia Cambogia is one such product that made claims that people could eat everything they wanted and still lose weight. What's in it for them?

- Lose weight - don't bother exercising - eat what you like.

Isn't that what people really want? Of course it is, but the problem is that many of the producers have used extracts in such small proportions they do nothing to help people to lose weight. Where it all goes wrong is when the advertisements show photographs that have been vetted. It casts doubt on the product's efficacy. There are complaints about the products and when that happens, it also begs the question, "What's in it for me?" especially at the prices being advertised. Complaints are lodged about being "conned" into having money taken from bank accounts at regular intervals without the purchaser having been made aware of the commitment.

Copywriters have to be careful about claims made in advertisements and most sellers of Garcinia Cambogia are quite careful, while others hide in the small print of those commitments. Can it make you slimmer? Cleverly worded copywriting tells you there is scientific evidence to support that fact. The raising of serotonin levels is supposed to give people better sleep and it's a known fact that people who sleep correctly actually do burn calories during sleep. If you were to interview people about how convincing the advertising is to them, however, there are those who question getting something without actually doing anything – so perhaps that sector of the public who are skeptics will keep away from the product because they don't see anything in it for them, other than spending money on something that may or may not work.

Copywriting has to take all of these potential customers into consideration and try to convince them all of the benefits of a product. Unfortunately, before and after photographs that are definitely taken from different angles and with the camera posed in different positions doesn't help the copywriting to be convincing. Thus, the whole package including imagery should form part of the storytelling done by the copywriter.

Use of clever, brief wording is great. Have you seen some of the chemical names introduced into beauty product advertising? There are some amazingly convincing ones, but be sure of what you are saying. It's important the customer buying the product believes in it rather than using it once and becoming very disappointed and disillusioned with the results they obtained.

In the adverts discussed in an earlier chapter, you can see quite clearly what's in it for people who gained from adverts for the following:

Farmers – The words of the advert meant their hard work was recognized and rewarded by the product.

Wonga Loans – The advert made it look like consumers could trust the old folks with the loans they wanted and that they were a no-fuss, easy payout loan for people who were short of cash.

The Cheerios Advert – This focused on enjoying the product during family time, which is what many homes lack these days due to work pressure. If a child can get up in the middle of the night to be with his father, doesn't he deserve to have Cheerios?

So many of the adverts we see on television these days are targeted to a specific audience and it is easy to see which audience that is from watching the adverts. Families are high on the list because these are spenders for everyday needs. All products that fall into this category are perfect products to aim toward those that will buy those product types. The point is they will buy the type that has the advert appeal over brands that do not.

Then you get home owners. They want good value for their home. They want something that makes their home unique. They want to feel their interior design is first rate, even if it isn't, and advertising aimed at homeowners carries this message. Look at the IKEA adverts. They make everything look so easy for the homeowner. It is easy for the homeowner because all they have to do is spend the money and IKEA provides modern, popular styling.

What's in it for the consumer is also covered by beauty ads that have the slogan "because I am worth it" written all over the ads. That makes a woman, even one who is poor or has little resources, buy products because it makes her feel special. She may even go without other things to ensure she gets what she feels she deserves.

Now look at adverts that are aimed at parents through children. What is inevitably in it for the consumer is that their children can keep up with other kids and they can have a relatively quiet life after Christmas or after birthdays, but advertisers don't stop there. You then have all the special occasions during the year with which to contend. Did your kid get the biggest Easter egg? How about on Father's day? How much did your TV advertising play in what you bought for him? We've even gone to such an extent that Valentine's Day isn't just for lovers anymore. Kids are encouraged to send parents Valentine's Day cards and even parents to send them to their kids. The world is crazy but you when put one idea forward that gives the hungry public what they are looking for, the rest will quickly follow suit. The idea of getting away from the rat race is such a popular one among people who feel the commercial world is letting them down. You hear about people escaping and moving "off the grid" but how much of that is real and how much of it is copywriting? The tiny house idea was popularized by TV and little did viewers know that behind this scheme offering mortgage-free living, companies were out there building tiny homes to offer at expensive prices. Whatever you read about in the media is, in effect, copywriting, especially if it has a slant to makes you consider spending money.

Knowing all of this, you need to hone your skills and make products sound as if they meet all the needs of the public who are willing to spend money to achieve whatever it is that the product offers. The No No campaign was a clever one aiming at the needs of women to get rid of facial hair. Since I have never known anyone that owns one of these, I had to decide whether the advertisement had merit. The makers guaranteed if you don't like the results that you get, your money would be refunded. That's pretty powerful copy because the public is left feeling the market is a safe one and they cannot possibly be ripped off.

Exercise: Look at items around your home and try to write a description of an item that would appeal to people looking to buy whatever it is. It can be anything from pharmaceutical products to washing detergent. All you are doing is practicing descriptions that show the public what's in it for them.

Chapter 12

What's in it for the Copywriter?

You may not be aware of this but some of the best-paid writers on the market don't even have their names on their work. These are copywriters. These are people who, behind the scenes, use their skills in language to persuade the public. Dan Kennedy is purported to earn millions per year in consulting and advertising work for his clients. He isn't the only one. You may not even have heard of his name, but that's not unusual. In the copywriting world, you won't experience fame unless you want to write about it and teach others your tricks. In general, copywriters are paid good money to produce outstanding results.

Let's look at some more typical earnings related to copywriting because the amount you can earn may be better than what you are now earning as a writer and you may be clever enough with your words to make copywriting your specialty. It really depends upon what you want in the way of a job. A part-timer can earn good hourly money for copywriting, but if you want to be like Dan Kennedy, you need to have a regular string of clients who come back to you regularly. I have ten such clients, which is enough to keep you going part time, as long as they are continually putting out information on websites or creating advertisements. My clients are active, so that's good money. Most part-timers can expect to earn around $15,000 just for working perhaps an hour or so a day. Up the ante and work full time and expect to triple that figure until you have an established reputation. When you have got a reputation for producing great copy, you can ask for more. If you are devoted to working for an agency or ad company, expect to earn more.

The thing I like the most about copywriting is you are left to use your imagination to lure the client into believing in your work. You are given a set time scale and when you present your ideas, sometimes these are presented via meetings. What you get from these meetings is very valuable input. I found that collaborating really does open your eyes to the ways other people see things, which is vital as a copywriter. If you don't see how farmers live their lives, how could you have written the advertisement for the trucks we mentioned before?

Every single person is a potential client for a product. Thus, seeing the product how others potentially see it helps you to write for a wider audience and thus increase the popularity of the product. One company that I wrote for provided software that dealt with payments over the Internet. I thought that I was aiming at big businesses and that the service was aimed specifically at them. When I learned in a meeting that the company was specifically targeting small companies because these were easy for them to handle and also increased their reputation, I changed the copy and we hit the target on the nail. Without consulting others, however, I may have made the mistake of providing limited copy.

If you are an imaginative writer and are good at fixing your writing to suit your client, then this may be the ideal career. However, if you are vain in your writing and believe what you wrote is the best and are unwilling to work on it, perhaps you need to concentrate your efforts somewhere with faster turn-over. Perhaps the news industry may give you the instant platform you demand.

The Kind of Person Who Fits in Well with Copywriting

You will need good English skills. If you don't have a wide vocabulary, you need to increase it before you even consider applying. Copywriters have to be flexible in their approach and be able to substitute words at the flip of a hat because they don't give the producer of the advert the right sound or the right amount of syllables. I have been asked to do this several times. Widening your vocabulary is essential.

You also have to be a people person. Those who hide away with their words are not the most astute at being able to get the message out to the masses. You need to understand the demographics of the country at whom you are aiming, the political stance and also a little about the kind of culture you are aiming advertising at. You may benefit from Neuro Linguistic training if you are aiming to work abroad because the nuances in the way people accept what's written may be different. The wider the scope of your understanding, the better.

You need to be someone who works well under stress. Sometimes, you are asked to produce copy very quickly and this may be replacement copy for something that someone else has produced. You also need to be a person who has a great imagination. Look at the most popular advertisements on YouTube and you will see there is no question that sense of humor and imagination are prerequisites for this type of career.

You also need to be able to persuade potential employers from the minute you hit the interview room. If you haven't got a background in copywriting but think your future could be in that line of work, you need to show examples of your thoughts to interviewers.

In one advertising agency, I used slogans I had made up for different products even though I never got to work on advertising those products. What I was showing them was what I was capable of producing. I remember being very animated in my explanation of one slogan. I actually acted out the parts and I had the interviewers in hysterics. They want fun new stuff and if you think about it, TV has been spouting off advertisements for so long now, getting new material is getting harder and harder for advertising companies. If you can give yourself a head start by showing your originality that goes a long way toward helping you get the job.

If you want to be a good copywriter, always look to improve your use of English so you can describe things. The best way possible to improve your use of language is to read a lot of material. This widens your vocabulary but it also shows you how authors are able to add color to their descriptions. Good quality authors can weave a whole tapestry of color into what they write. They can suck you into their stories and show you a lot of tricks you would never learn had you not taken the time to become a great reader. Be enthralled, be inspired, but most of all learn from the language you read. Reading is the best tool for people who want to make their living in the land of writing of any kind, including copywriting.

Chapter 13

So How Do You Become a Great Copywriter?

Skills

As a copywriter, one of the required skills is to write effective copy that converts its readers. Sadly, a lot of copywriters do not invest enough time to develop this skill. Yes, I did use the word "develop," because whether you realize it or not, everyone has a creative gene. The only difference is if you are doing something to improve that part in you. The good news is your creative wiring only needs a little ignition, and getting yourself influenced by experts can do that.

So, if you think it was just an accident you came across this job, think again. Maybe you only need a little inspiration. It's about high time to sharpen your skill in order for you to keep up with others and survive and thrive.

Let me share with you some of the most significant skills that a copywriter must have:

Know Your Audience

What is the info you need to know from your audience? Do you need to know their age range? Do you need to know in which area they live? Do you have to know what they do for a living? These things might help you know them on a personal note but knowing the answers won't be enough to inspire you to write copy that will compel their emotions and make them interested in reading your ad.

In order to get to write something captivating, we need to traverse the deep recesses of a customer's mind. The brain behind the idea of figuring out what the customer is thinking in order to write persuasive copy is a person named Lajos Egri. According to his book, *The Art of Dramatic Writing*, there is but one simple rule: "Know your characters and you'll know your story." Egri's book is regarded as one of the best books about playwriting but you'll see that what he said in his book has pretty much the same effects when used in copywriting.

Here are a couple of things we can learn from Lajos Egri and use in copywriting:

What Your Reader Wants the Most is to be IMPORTANT

Egri said the number one desire that motivates all characters is to be important. Even the simplest actions are a sign of making efforts to be significant in this world. We dress up for a date, we strive to get a promotion, we make sure our children are in the best health, etc. And why do we do these things? Why do we make these a part of our goals? It's because we want to be noticed, we want to gain some respect, we want to be loved and cared for in return. And when we are able to do so, we see it as a barometer on how important we are for these people.

Going back to advertising, how do companies let their customers know they are precious? You can make your customer feel valued by acknowledging their presence, letting them into a secret or a tip, respecting their time, and helping them keep their dignity. When you are aware what makes your customer feel valued and important, you can be assured that your copy will turn out to be something that will benefit the company.

Remember, knowing your customer's desire for importance is just the beginning. Without digging deeper into the murky waters, you won't be able to fully grasp what's in your customer's mind.

Your Reader Is INSECURE and You Have to Find Out Why

I agree with Egri when he said, "no one is wholly satisfied with themselves, because if people were satisfied and happy, no one would ever do anything." Insecurities are what bring about dissatisfaction. We are insecure about our weight, so we buy dieting capsules and juices. We are insecure about wearing old clothes to a friend's party, so we buy a new outfit though the old one still fits perfectly. We are insecure about not knowing as much as our next door neighbor so we enroll in a Japanese class. All of those insecurities are what push us to pursue activities that will somehow try to gain us some importance or added value.

That is exactly the point when writing persuasive copy—to hit your entire customer's insecurities when you are selling the same product. You have to know the reason for those insecurities as well. For example, a lot of people may decide to attend the gym but for different reasons. One guy might be motivated to have a toned body and to develop muscles in order to impress ladies, while another person may be motivated because of a chronic disease and the fear he might miss out on a lot of things in life if he doesn't keep in shape. In such a case, you'll see the same fitness product may benefit both people but the writing approach may not. If you want to create copy that will touch your customers deeply, you need to see their fears and their goals.

Vital Clues Could Just Be in The Past

Customer profiles are always kept up to date. It focuses on their details at the present: where they live now, what problems they have today, and so on and so forth. But according to Egri, if you really want to understand your character, you need to go back into his past. You have to know the events that happened in between yesterday and today that made your customers who they are today.

You have to know what your customers have been through. What events have made them turn out to be part of your target market? If you are helping small-scale business owners, know how they get to where they are now. What's their history? Have they always been self-employed?

As you take time to figure out this kind of information from your audience, you will have a better view of the values your customers have lived by. It will also allow you to shape your copy into one that will best fit your audience.

Conflicts Uncover Your Audience's Real Character

According to Egri, people's real characteristics are revealed during conflict. Know what conflicts your audience is facing.

There may be conflicts that are too obvious. Usually, what happens is that there's an event that becomes a problem, which need to be resolved by a reaction. For example, you need to get somewhere but your car suddenly breaks down. Now you need to get a mechanic. Or your water pipes burst and you don't want water damage, so you call a plumber to get things fixed.

Other conflicts are subtler and need a closer look to be figured out. Let's say a business owner wants a classy looking website, saying she wants to look important to her customers. At first glance, you can't really see where the conflict lies. But look closely and you will see she is about to start up a business and she is a technology novice. She doesn't have much funding to get a design company but she can't do her own design because she is not familiar with that technology.

If you did not dig in, you might offer the business owner a wrong solution to her problem. But if you were able to see this and understand where the conflict lies, you would be able to plan the right content to reach this customer and not just advertise web designs that are highly affordable.

You don't need to know your target market's individual stories but having no idea at all as to the conflict the majority of them are facing, you won't get to understand where they are really coming from, and reading their character might be a great challenge to undertake.

Know Their Limits and How Far Are They Willing to Go

In fiction stories, you should know if your characters are prepared to risk going on a risky adventure, commit a heinous crime, or disown their family in order to achieve their dreams. The same is true with your customers. You have to know their limits. You have to know how far they are willing to go.

As an advertiser, you need to know what your audience is willing to do in order to resolve conflicts. You have to find out how much they would be willing to cash out. You have to figure out whether they are willing to shop around or if they are the type who buys on impulse. You have to know the extent of their desperation in trying to solve their problem. You have to know how much time they are willing to give to get it solved. Is it okay for the problem to be solved in a matter of days or weeks? Or does the problem need to be resolved ASAP? You have to know how willing they are to work with you over your competitors.

The right research can get you to open up new approaches in presenting an offer to your prospects. Should you discover your customers love to shop around and take time to read a lot about a product before finally considering what to buy, you will have the chance to create copy that caters to this need.

Finding out your customer's real character is not something that can be done overnight; its tedious and time consuming. Egri himself shared how he would spend hours to plot questions and answer scenarios with characters, create a range of different back stories, and get himself to imagine how each character would react to various events and opposing personalities.

It's good to know that with these same principles Egri presented, and despite knowing your audience is real, you may use the same strategies to find out what your target audiences have in mind. And with that, you can find out their soft spot.

Mastering the Art of Active Listening

The goal of effective copy is to communicate effectively. And how does effective communication begin? By knowing your target audience. The primary way to do this is by listening.

Listening is more than just merely hearing someone out. When we listen, we are able to obtain vital information. When we listen, we are able to understand better. Finally, when we listen, we learn.

As a copywriter, you need to listen to your audience. Based on Steven Covey's book entitled *The 7 Habits of Highly Effective People*, one needs to first seek to understand before being understood. In order for you to be understood by your target audience, you need to understand them first. Know what your audience really wants. Stop assuming what they want, dig into the facts, research, and listen.

And how would you know unless you ask? It's surprising to know many marketers fail in this aspect of asking for feedback from their audience. And worse, some do not listen to what is said. It's very simple logic: if you don't listen, you won't understand. And if you fail to understand your audience, how can you give them what they want? You must keep in mind that your goal is first and foremost to listen with the intention to help, not listen in order to gain. Take time to listen and your audience will put their trust in you.

Learn How to Speak Well

After you have heard your customer, you also need to sharpen your skills in learning how to speak well. A good marketer must have the skills to play with words in order to get the interest of his target market. When you know how to speak well, you will be able to convince anyone, or sell ice to Eskimos, as they say. It's not enough you write good copy; you need to write good copy with results.

On the bright side, this is a skill that can be learned. To be able to speak well, you only need to know the right language to use. And you can do that by expanding your knowledge through reading. Here are some tips on how to choose the right words to speak and mean well:

- **Pick words your target audience uses.** Make them feel like you are talking with them by using the very same language they use.

- **Choose precise words.** It is encouraged to make your thesaurus your writing buddy to inspire your writing. Be careful, though, as some synonyms still have slightly different meanings.

- **Use sensory words.** Sensory words are powerful because they allow your readers to see, hear, taste, smell, or feel what you are telling them.

- **Make every word relevant.** Less is more, but not so all the time. Sometimes, it's helps to add a word or two to make your sentence appear more relevant and specific.

Don't Beat Around the Bush

Be brief. Don't beat around the bush. When you are writing a short form of copy, skip the stories. Just get on with the facts. When you don't say your point right away, the tendency is for your reader to get bored or impatient. So say your words well, but say them quickly.

Don't Put a Lid on Creativity

The difference between copy that converts and copy that doesn't lie is how creative it is. Just as previously mentioned, everyone has creativity but the trouble is in keeping creative juices flowing. And once you have tapped into that creativity, you can learn to use it every time you need it.

Some copywriters dislike the thought of making creativity a special ingredient in crafting good copy. Others prefer to call it 'remarkable' instead of 'creative.' Being creative doesn't hurt. Just as Carl Ally said, "The creative person wants to be a know-it-all. He wants to know about all kinds of things—ancient history, nineteenth century mathematics, and current manufacturing techniques and hog futures. Because he never knows when these ideas might come together to form a new idea. It may happen six minutes later, or six months, or six years. But he has faith that it will happen."

Again, to be inspired and get your creative juices flowing, it will help to read everything you can. Even read topics that may be outside your expertise.

Make a Sale

Sometimes, copywriters are so obsessed with creating copy they miss the whole point of why they are doing what they are doing. Keep in mind the point of writing good copy is to sell. In truth, there are no right or wrong ways to sell. There may be principles advertisers have deemed the 'best' ones because of having experienced how they worked for them, but there is nothing really specific as to assure you that in this span of time you will get your ROI. Everyone has a distinct style in selling.

And because of having different styles and gimmicks, the battle lies in how persistent a marketer is. However, it's sad to know a lot of people do not appreciate or understand this. As an advertiser, you need to have the spine to try and try until you discover the one that works for you. Once you have found out your customer's sweet spot, everything will be easier. If you want to be an effective copywriter, study all the strategies in selling.

Study What SEO Is

Understanding what SEO is might sound a little too technical. SEO actually stands for Search Engine Optimization. Big words, right? But you don't need to be some sort of genius to figure this out. SEO is basically the process of getting traffic from search results through search engines. As a copywriter and an online marketer, you will have the advantage in your craft if you try to learn this important skill.

Be Real

People look for authenticity. Nowadays, authenticity is a rare find, especially on the Internet. It seems as if 50% of websites are a scam. How do you keep yourself real? Stop pretending you are someone you are not. If you are a pretentious copywriter, know someone will blow your cover one day and that won't be a very nice sight to see. Be real! Believe me, being true to yourself, your story, and sharing it is more powerful than you think.

Research

Much of what you will be doing is background investigation to find out the market to which the product is being targeted. That gives you more work, by finding out what lesser products the competition is offering, you will be able to exploit this knowledge within your copywriting material. It's not as if you have to say:

"This product is better than this specific product."

You just need to be aware of claims being made by competitors and little by little, feed the public doubt about what competitors are offering. The public knows the advertisements. There's no need to slam someone, but there are ways to show how your product does better and when you manage to do that, you win. If you want to become a copywriter, find a company that produces an item you believe in because that makes your work much easier. Look through listings from advertising companies, as they are always on the lookout for good copywriters for their client base.

Show ideas. Have a portfolio of your own original concepts for known products. Yes, this means work, but it also means an advertising agency can see you have grasped the idea of all of the points mentioned in previous chapters. If you haven't, you might as well become an Internet Poet with the rest of the "wannabe" writers. Copywriting takes hard work, research, and originality. It doesn't come naturally to everyone, but those who are good at it earn very good money indeed. The pay scales for copywriters in the US are between $44,631 and $71,000, which are not wages for a writer to scoff at. You need to understand your chosen medium.

For example, if you are aiming at billboards, these are different than TV adverts. If you are advertising on the side of a bus, it's different than radio advertising. Thus, your portfolio should include different mediums and show you understand the differences.

Ask yourself who will see this advert and how long they will see it for. Billboards may only be seen for a few moments as a vehicle is passing, as may those adverts on the sides of public transport. Thus, the message has to be exceedingly powerful to meet the masses head on. The call to action or the "What are you waiting for?" message incorporated into an advertisement encourages the public to buy, but that isn't the only angle from which you need to write. You also need to cover the manufacturer from false claims, as this casts doubt. You must also make sure you don't give away too much information. It's about brevity.

Pitching Like a Pro

A pro will pitch when being interviewed. A pro will know the type of companies an advertising company represents. A pro will be prepared with a comparable portfolio even if that portfolio is hypothetical and made for interview purposes.

A pro will also be quick on the mark and be able to come up with slogans that fit circumstances. In one interview, I was asked for an on-the-spot slogan for a product that was placed in my hands. I had never seen the product before the interview. Such a scenario can happen. In my case, it was something that appealed to my sense of humor and I was able to pitch my answer like a pro in order to impress the interviewers with my ability to play on words. People enjoy that kind of thing and I knew that the words I had chosen were suitable for the particular product, the kind of audience it would be aimed at, and that the interviewers would be suitably amused.

Copywriting is a serious job but it's one that can use serious humor. If you have a sharp sense of wit, you may be able to produce very good copy using your sense of humor to guide you. However, don't use it to your detriment. Look on YouTube and see which advertisements were banned from television because they were deemed unsuitable for viewers.

Perhaps your take on a product may just be tempting enough to show the advertising company pitching really isn't a problem and there is a huge amount of imagination waiting to be unleashed. Often companies see ideas in meetings that don't meet the mark, but yours might. If you still want to be a copywriter, it's time to pitch like a pro to become one.

Ethics

Just like journalists, an effective copywriter follows a code of ethics when writing. Good copy cannot be considered worth the read without ethical content, whether it's a creative article or a freelance job. With an array of new types of media emerging in the writing industry today, it is vital a copywriter is well versed in journalism ethics and standards as well as a media code of ethics.

The following are important aspects to consider in writing:

<u>Honesty</u>

Being truthful and accurate is one of the feats of an ethically written article. Copywriting should never be separate from sharing only fact-based information. Coming up with accurate content is one of the responsibilities of a copywriter.

While it is true copywriting clients may ask you to write in different tones per topic: edgy, funny, a little light-hearted, hip, totally serious, etc., a copywriter should not depart from the truth.

While it's great to perfect your writing tone, sometimes there is a possibility for you to be perceived in a different light. To make it easier to be understood, writing tone is a verbalized non-verbal communication. It's similar to a hand gesture to stress something important, a raised brow to show emotions, or a crooked smile, only that in copy it's put into a combination of words, phrases, and punctuations. However, using tone to drive a desired impression fails at times because even like-minded individuals sometimes don't share the same perception. What sounds edgy to you may sound immature or arrogant to another person. What's funny may be perceived as rather unsympathetic to another reader.

For this reason, every copywriter must aim for honesty and clarity rather than ambiguity. Of course, every writer wants to be on top of his game and would like to sound unique and striking, which is what makes it a tough call. At the end of the day, honesty still beats up puffery. It's still making readers understand your message is more important than trying to make them impressed with all of those big words. The following are reasons why you should make honesty and clarity on top of your list as a copywriter:

- Honesty is a universally accepted tone everyone respects.

- Being ambiguous in your writing tone can create a bad impression and damage your brand.

- What was once 'hype' can also eventually turn out to be tiresome.

- The clearer your message, the more customers you'll gain.

- When in print, it is *what is said* that matters and not *how it is said*.

Words can have different shades of meaning. As a copywriter, should you bend or stretch the truth just because you can? A great copywriter is one who writes not only effective articles, but writes those based in truth. He emphasizes on a brand's real strengths and does not cover it up with fake ones. Honesty as a writing ethic expresses the truth as a benefit for its readers.

Plagiarism

Avoiding plagiarism is one of the most important writing ethics. Although it would take a lot of explaining to define the grounds for plagiarism, it is easier to simply define plagiarism as theft. It is the act of stealing another person's ideas or words, with or without the intent of doing so, and not paying proper attribution to the individual who owns those ideas.

In copywriting, plagiarism is using another person's writing. It can be copying some parts of a previously published article or study without providing a proper citation. According to the Merriam-Webster online dictionary, as gathered and presented by plagiarism.org, plagiarism is:

- stealing and passing off (the ideas or words of another) as one's own
- using (another's production) without crediting the source
- committing literary theft
- presenting as new and original an idea or product derived from an already existing source

In most cases of plagiarism, the perpetrator alleges to have duplicated another person's work without knowing. To put it simply, they believe it's not their fault at all. The following are some of the common excuses for plagiarism:

1. Misunderstanding. A lot of times, people do not know the weight of plagiarism, or even what the act is in and of itself. A common excuse is someone doesn't believe he or she has done anything wrong. This is often the scenario, especially in academic setting.

2. Lapse of judgment. This is common among journalists and researchers. They admit they made a mistake of committing plagiarism but promise not to do it again a second time. It's an admission they know they did wrong but went for it despite their knowledge.

3. Blaming it on the sources. Because of advancing technology, it's easy for anyone to get information with a single click. Although most plagiarists would not admit it, many of us think because there's so much information over the web, copying small portions of someone else's work occasionally won't hurt.

But what about self-plagiarism? Writers often reason that because they are the authors themselves, they can use and reuse their previous works as they want and not be guilty of plagiarism because it's their own words. However, though this is still under debate, self-plagiarism should be avoided because it may reflect upon a publisher's copyright.

Here are ways you can avoid plagiarism:

Learn to paraphrase. Make sure throughout your writing and research process, you read and understand your research to the point you can put it into your own words and not copy it verbatim.

Know how citations work. Aside from paraphrasing, using citations is also an effective way to avoid plagiarism. Not being able to properly cite may lead to plagiarism, so it's important to follow the right document formatting guidelines.

Quote your source. If you cannot avoid copying more than two words in a row verbatim, the way to avoid plagiarism is by quoting.

Cite quotes. Citing a quote is not the same as citing a paraphrased resource. It includes the addition of a page number or a paragraph number.

Cite even your own material. To avoid self-plagiarism, you need to cite even your own words, should they appear in a different publication. Treat it as though you are citing someone else's work.

Integrity

As a copywriter, one should be careful not to create biased reviews and content. The type of content created solely to skew perception does not convey the truth. If you are writing out of your own bias, then what you are writing about may not be truthful, but only out of your personal opinion. As the word implies, integrity is standing on strong moral principles, in decency, truthfulness, and fairness. Integrity in copywriting points us back to number one—honesty.

Why is it important to have integrity in writing? It's simple—how you write is a reflection of yourself as a person. Integrity encompasses a lot of things. It reflects the things you value as a copywriter. If you look at writing as a profession and you highly respect the code of ethics and standards as a copywriter, you write with the goal to convey only what is factual and impartial.

Reliability

A good copywriter is one who can deliver copy persuasive enough to draw people to your brand within the agreed upon time. A copywriter is supposed to be an investment to a company, not a liability. Therefore, one must be really meticulous in finding the right person for the job. According to Rachel Miller, the following is what one can do to get a reliable copywriter:

Create a shortlist. There may be thousands of freelance copywriters out there of different specializations. You can (1) search through the Internet for professional copywriters in your area. You may also (2) ask around from your friends and colleagues for recommendations. Lastly, you can (3) inquire from your industry's association or your local business support for seasoned copywriters they have been in contact with in the past.

Schedule a one-on-one interview. After getting a couple of interested copywriters to join your team, it is essential to choose the best person for the job. Asking a lot of relevant questions during one-on-one interviews could do this. Make sure the candidate knows what he is doing and what things the company is looking for in a copywriter.

Opt for the best match. You can't just pick anyone who is familiar with the kind of sector your company is involved with. If you want to make sure you are rooting for the right and reliable copywriter, find someone who fits the style your brand handles. It must be someone with the right knack to persuade both your current and potential customers.

They must write in the right tone of voice your customers are interested in. They must be able to produce good copy.

What good copy looks like:

- Easy to navigate; not complicated

- Has catchy headings that persuade you to read

- Conveys a clear message

- Uses minimal jargon

- Has consistency in style; perfect spelling and punctuation

- Key details all intact

Kindness

A copywriter ought to write persuasive copy by stressing great qualities of a brand, not by criticizing a competitor's weakness in order to say his brand is better. A copywriter who writes ethical content will by no means slander another individual or group to lose their customer's trust.

Chapter 14

Trade Secrets to Effective Copywriting

SEO

We have already covered a lot of territory and have had you working through various exercises to try and help you to make your copywriting more effective. However, you do need to understand more about the ways in which you can make your copy get the results companies desire. With the Internet being such a huge market for copywriters, you do need to understand a little about how much different SEO or search engine optimization means to the words that you write. If you don't use SEO, you should. The words you use in your work are what are used by Search Engines to find you the right audience. Thus, keywords are associated with the product are used within the text to draw in readers. However, don't make the mistake of thinking your work needs to be stacked full of these. If you overdo it, your work will sound unnatural and will be dismissed by people who don't want to plough through a lot of nonsense to find out what they want to know.

Headlines

Writers in all fields of writing are taught about the importance of headlines and this is very important when it comes to writing copy. If you lose the interest of the reader in the opening of your articles, you fail your client. You also lose the opportunity of winning the loyalty of potential purchasers.

Learn to discipline yourself

Writers in all styles of writing need to make sure they have sufficient sleep in order to be able to start a job with a fresh frame of mind. The best ideas come from those who have this discipline because they don't take baggage from other things into the room with them when they settle down to work. They have an organized area in which to work without interruption. It should be an inspiring space. If you have not yet learned not to multi-task, then you need to get into the habit of concentrating on what it is you are doing to become a good copywriter. Yes, you may do research to give you an idea of what the competition is doing. Yes, this part of the work helps you to keep your work cutting-edge and up to date. However, once that is done, you need to stop letting yourself become distracted.

One of the best copywriters I know is someone who practices meditation. She tells me this allows her to work uninterrupted and helps her to sharpen her mind for her writing. If you think this will help you, or are a person who tends to prevaricate and mess around before actually getting down to the task, then perhaps enrolling in a class will help you. The idea is that when you tackle the copywriting project, your mind is totally on the job at hand and is allowed to work in a very creative way because you are literally freeing your mind from thinking about other things.

Targeting the reader's emotions

If you think people generally make purchases based on financial considerations or logic, then you haven't understood how the buying public sees things. Most will be affected by how their emotions drive them toward buying a specific item. Thus, your copywriting needs to bear this in mind and show those reading your copy the ways in which the client can derive emotional comfort from what you are selling. Clever copywriters lull their readers into a sense of security and it is that security of emotions that will pull in more potential purchasers than anything else. Always try to remember this. In fact, if you go back on your briefs from earlier chapters, read through them and find out if it was something you got right. If it wasn't, try rewriting the briefs using the emotional pull needed to get people to be happy to spend their money.

Pleasing your client

The client is going to pay you for the work you produce, so you have to balance the way you react so you finish the brief and also please the client. Since the client can either "yay" or "nay" your work, it's vital you have the client on your side. The best way to make sure that this happens is to have a meeting with your client and ask the client to describe the way he or she sees the product or service you are describing. This also tells you a lot about what your client will expect from your finished copy.

Using the argument of logic

If you close your eyes and think about the world's top products, you will find the reason you believe them to be top products is because you believe the products are superior to others within the same market. For example, people think instantly of Apple and see this as a leader in the computer field. Apple has been selling its products to people who want to own the best. Their slick explanation to clients on their website shows them logically that the investment in their products is wise and what they are being offered cannot be bettered. I actually like the idea that Apple standardizes the price structure and that you are unlikely to find the products in cheap stores. It backs up their assertion of being the best. The problem is that we are lulled into buying all kinds of things. It can be rather disappointing to find the same thing can be purchased cheaply simply by shopping around.

When you write copy for a product, you not only need to explain why people need the product, but how it improves people's lives. Whether you use the storytelling method or simply describe the product in a drier manner is your client's choice. Be candid. Do make comparisons if that's what is needed and be completely truthful so people can trust your words. Once you do, you will gain more sales because people will trust what you have said and have confidence in the product. There are thousands of opportunities waiting out there for someone who can use their vocabulary in such a way as to describe the product and make people relate to it.

Increase your vocabulary

As a copywriter, make sure you are on top of your game by being able to use words that give people a level of confidence in the product they have never had before. If you do decide to use simple vocabulary for a simple audience, make the copy something memorable so it will stay in their minds long after they have switched off their computer or turned off their TV. It's a good idea to do crosswords often because these are the source of great words you can use in future copy. One of the best crosswords is one that truly makes you think beyond the obvious. If, for example, you are writing copy about food, what words – beyond the obvious – could you use to describe that food? You have a responsibility to provide interesting and stimulating copy that gains popularity simply because of the quality of the written word. Unlike all other kinds of writing, copywriting has a specific purpose:

to see a product or service by making writing fit the appropriate market and target audience.

Step out of your own comfort zone by increasing your vocabulary and you will be able to produce original copy. Add a little humor where appropriate and make sure everything you write is edited again and again until you are happy with the product. Great copy comes from clever ideas but it is rare that the first attempt will be the one you will use when presenting your ideas to a client. Improve what you write by using a wider range of words and memorable phrases, then edit and snip until the message is astute and capable of conveying confidence to all who read it.

Conclusion

Despite the overview of this book, you must take it further if you want to become the best copywriter you can. Throughout the chapters, the tips that were given were to help you to see copywriting isn't just writing a flowery description about a product. It's about convincing a target audience they can't live without having a certain product. It's about belief in the product. It's also about being able to express all of this in such a way that your message targets the audience most likely to buy the product you are selling.

Look into the competition and find their weaknesses. The iPad advertisers did this perfectly, in that they knew the public still suspiciously views the innovative and complicated systems produced by iPad competitors. Instead of describing their system in a complex way, they demonstrated it as totally suitable to everyone's lifestyle in a stylish way. That's clever, honest copywriting, and it hit the target audience in a way no one could have anticipated. The new iPad Air has equally taken the imagination of the public by storm by offering lightness the old iPad didn't offer. However, you'd be hard pressed to make an iPad user part with the technology once you made the sale.

We told a similar story about cut-price airlines and how luxury airlines exploited the fact that "no frills" may not be what a discerning traveler is looking for. A good copywriter knows the following:

- The benefits of the product to target population
- The competition and what it offers in comparison with your product
- The medium by which advertising will be spread
- The time limits or constraints the copywriter must to work within
- The public sector at which the adverts are aimed

Once you add having a great vocabulary coming up with brief but imaginative copy people automatically associate with the product, you will have sufficient information to persuade the public to buy. Look back at the catchphrases we shared with you, as some of these are so typical of what is being used to lure the public these days. Some of these will last for generations because consumers believe in what they are investing.

You are selling a brand. Think Nike and the catchphrase that instantly comes to mind is, "Just Do It." If that doesn't push people who are having trouble making up their minds, then nothing will. Brands depend upon copywriters to come up with the right copy to sell and the examples shown to you in this book are first-rate examples.

Disneyland is still selling tickets based on the fact that it's purported to be "the happiest place on Earth." This appeals to both grown-ups and kids alike, who are seeking out an adventure taking them away from the doldrums of normalcy and into another world where people are all happy.

All of this is a lot for one person to work on but it's all part and parcel of working as a copywriter. If you feel you have the imagination and are able to play with words in order to pass on a message, then perhaps this is the career for you. With a Bachelor's Degree in Advertising, followed by or during which freelance work is undertaken, you stand a good chance to become one of the best. Keep up to date with current trends and you will find the work is rewarding as you experience success.

Freelance work is always available, though if you wish to have the security of being employed by an advertising company or a public relations company, this should be your goal. Online companies are offering jobs to copywriters, but be aware you may lose copyright of written work, as clients paying for work tend to take that as part of the deal. Mind you, that's not much different to working for an agency, because the agency takes copyright on what their employees produce. If you are happy with that, you can think of this as being a practice run to actually working in an advertising environment with the agency taking all of the credit for the work you produce.

It's a very satisfying career and one that suits people who are not afraid of new things. It would also suit those who are open to changes and working for different clients with different needs. Specializing in a field is also possible, such as cosmetics, industry, etc., and your specialist area could also be backed up by qualifications that show your knowledge of the product range. However, never close the entrance door to opportunity. The best copywriting I ever did was on a product I actually knew nothing about before undergoing all of the investigation needed to be able to produce. The fact that the product was new to me opened up new avenues of exploration and perhaps it was the freshness of approach that made it such a success.

I wish you well in copywriting. You may have decided by now copywriting isn't for you. You may not want your writing associated with branding or product sales but for those who do, this is a rewarding career move that gives a steady flow of work and great pay. You may not earn millions, but you will never know until you try. It's enjoyable, for every job is different, and you change your approach every time you have new copy to write, otherwise you get stale. If you are stuck in your ways as a writer, you can't expect to pitch like a pro, which is what copywriting is all about.

Copywriting takes your writing skills one step further than straight writing. Does that mean that you can't have heroes and heroines? Of course not. You only have to see the adverts on the television screen to know that even advertising copy allows you the benefit of creativity. Think of all the memorable advertisements you have ever seen and know that behind every one of them was a very clever copywriter who somehow got it right. If you can remember the advert, they did their job properly. That's what you need to be aiming for.

The adverts standing out in your mind or the copy you read on the Internet that struck a chord with you is clever copywriting. This book has many exercises and you will be able to go through them time and time again, choosing different products and objects to use. It pays to give yourself boring items as well as those that you find exciting because a good copywriter is able to make even the mundane sound necessary and exciting to the buying public. If you have spare time, pick up an object and try to describe it using all of the styles relevant to copywriting because all of the practice you get helps you to be able to change styles instantly to suit the market and the age range to whom you are aiming your copy. It's important to keep up to date with trends and to keep an eye on what's being offered by the competition at all times because this gives you an idea of the clichés to avoid. Often, bad copywriting shows up big time, which allows you to keep working within the parameters set by your client without making you look foolish or as if you have not understood the brief you have been given.

Made in the USA
Monee, IL
15 June 2021